The History of a Village Community in the Eastern Counties (Methwold). ... Illustrated ... by the author.

Joan Denny Gedge

The History of a Village Community in the Eastern Counties (Methwold). ... Illustrated ... by the author.
Gedge, Joan Denny
British Library, Historical Print Editions
British Library
1893
130 p. ; 4°.
10351.g.31.

The BiblioLife Network

This project was made possible in part by the BiblioLife Network (BLN), a project aimed at addressing some of the huge challenges facing book preservationists around the world. The BLN includes libraries, library networks, archives, subject matter experts, online communities and library service providers. We believe every book ever published should be available as a high-quality print reproduction; printed on- demand anywhere in the world. This insures the ongoing accessibility of the content and helps generate sustainable revenue for the libraries and organizations that work to preserve these important materials.

The following book is in the "public domain" and represents an authentic reproduction of the text as printed by the original publisher. While we have attempted to accurately maintain the integrity of the original work, there are sometimes problems with the original book or micro-film from which the books were digitized. This can result in minor errors in reproduction. Possible imperfections include missing and blurred pages, poor pictures, markings and other reproduction issues beyond our control. Because this work is culturally important, we have made it available as part of our commitment to protecting, preserving, and promoting the world's literature.

GUIDE TO FOLD-OUTS, MAPS and OVERSIZED IMAGES

In an online database, page images do not need to conform to the size restrictions found in a printed book. When converting these images back into a printed bound book, the page sizes are standardized in ways that maintain the detail of the original. For large images, such as fold-out maps, the original page image is split into two or more pages.

Guidelines used to determine the split of oversize pages:

- Some images are split vertically; large images require vertical and horizontal splits.
- For horizontal splits, the content is split left to right.
- For vertical splits, the content is split from top to bottom.
- For both vertical and horizontal splits, the image is processed from top left to bottom right.

HE HISTORY OF A VILLAGE COMMUNITY
IN THE EASTERN COUNTIES.

The History

OF

A VILDLAGE COMMUNITY

In the Eastern Counties.

BY THE

REV. J. DENNY GEDGE,

VICAR OF METHWOLD.

Illustrated with Anastatic Sketches in Pen and Ink

BY THE AUTHOR.

Norwich:
AGAS H. GOOSE, RAMPANT HORSE STREET.
1893.

DEDICATION.

LIGHT of our world, and Maker of our sight,
   By gift of Whom we see or know aught right,
Who only canst illumine,—oft as night
Of doubt or anguish hem us lonely quite
From all, save Thou appearest, making light
To rise up in our darkness. Patient Guide,
Who standest waiting, where to turn aside
Were waste of precious life; and bid'st us bide
To ask Thy counsel, since that Thou hast tried
Our journey, and the Pathway verified;
Who preachest all Thy lessons from the Rood,
That cruel bar, which seemed as it withstood
Thy road to glory and Thy People's good,
Till, climbing it, in Faith's full hardihood,
Thou reached'st Heaven again; so that who would
Come there to Thee, and share Thy kingliness
(For, of Thy Love, Thou offerest no less),
Must mount thereby, and learn so to repress
The fatal choice of unbroke selfishness,—
Be Thou our Light, our Guide, our Worthiness.

PREFACE.

THIS is only the work of a smatterer. I avow it freely, not without regret that it must be so, but without shame that it is so; for we country parsons, isolated as we are, many of us, by the ordering of Providence, from the great world, become in this way, almost perforce, either smatterers or gossips. My innate tendencies have relegated me to the former class. But I think I have hanselled here somewhat of a new idea in the treatment of Parish Histories; and ideas, as even worlds, must begin by being nebulous.

Methwold Vicarage,
    April, 1893.

ERRATA.

Page 12, line 19. For "door" *read* "low," *i.e.*, burial ground
  „ 59 „   5. For "her" grandmother, *read* "his."

LIST OF SUBSCRIBERS.

Amherst of Hackney, The Right Hon. Lord, Didlington Hall, Brandon.
Barnard, G. W. G., Esq., Surrey Street, Norwich.
Beevor, Miss L., The Limes, Weybridge.
Bensly, Dr., Registrar to the Lord Bishop of Norwich, Eaton, Norwich.
Birch, Rev. C. G. R., Brancaster Rectory, King's Lynn.
Birkbeck, H., Esq., J.P., Stoke Holy Cross, Norwich.
Bodley, Rev. Father, Oxburgh, Brandon, Norfolk.
Boileau, Sir Francis G. M., Bart., Ketteringham Park, Norwich.
Bolden, J. L., Esq., Office of the Duchy of Lancaster, London, W.C.
Brent, Cecil, Esq., F.R.A.S., 37, Palace Grove, Bromley, Kent.
Browne, Miss F. A., 5, Clifton Grove, Torquay, S. Devon.
Buxton, C. Louis, Esq., Bolwick Hall, Marsham.
Calvert, Rev. T., 15, Albany Villas, Hove, Brighton.
Carter, John, Esq., Manor House, Northwold.
Chapman, The Ven. Archdeacon, The Almonry, Ely.
Colman, J. J., Esq., M.P., Carrow House, Norwich.
Donne, W. Mowbray, Esq., 3, Gloucester Terrace, Hyde Park, London, W.
Elwin, C. N., Esq., M.A., Eckling Grange, East Dereham.
Engleheart, Sir J. Gardiner D., C.B., Office of the Duchy of Lancaster, London, W.C.
Ffolkes, Sir Wm. H. B., Bart., Hillington Hall, King's Lynn.
Frankau, H., Esq., 1, Elm Court, Temple, London, E.C.
Gedge, Mr. Johnson, Bromley, Kent.
Gedge, Sydney, Esq., M.P., 1, Old Palace Yard, Westminster.
Great Yarmouth Free Library (Mr. Wm. Carter).
Greenwell, Rev. Canon, F.R.A.S., Durham.
Griffith, Rev. H. T., Smallburgh Rectory, Norwich.
Gurdon, Sir Wm. Brampton, Grundisburgh Hall, Woodbridge.
Gurney, R. H., Esq., J.P., North Repps Hall, Cromer.
Haggard, H. Rider, Esq., Ditchingham House, Bungay.
Haggard, W. M. R., Esq., Bradenham Hall.
Hardie, E., Esq., Office of the Duchy of Lancaster, London, W.C.

Howell, Rev. Canon Hinds, Drayton Rectory, Norwich.
Hudson, Rev. W., Secretary of the Norfolk and Norwich Archæological Society.
Hutt, H. R. M., Esq., Wilton Rectory, Brandon.
Jarrold, W. F. T., Esq., Norwich.
Jarrold and Sons, Messrs., Norwich.
Last, Madame, 3, Maisons Saulnier, derrière Rue Voltaire, Genéve, Suisse.
Joy, Dr., Northwold, Brandon.
Legge, Rev. A. G., Elmham Vicarage, East Dereham.
le Strange, Hamon, Esq., Hunstanton Hall, Norfolk.
Lott, Rev. W. B., Barton Mills Rectory, Mildenhall.
Lubbock, Sir John, Bart., M.P., L.C.C., F.R.A.S.
Manchester, The Very Rev. the Dean of.
Marsham, Hon. Robert, 5, Chesterfield Street, Mayfair, London, W.
Morfill, Professor W. R., Professor of Slavonic Languages, Oxford.
Norfolk, His Grace the Duke of, Norfolk House, St. James' Square, S.W.
Norwich Free Library.
Orpen, Rev. Thos. H., Binnbrooke, Cambs.
Orpen, J. R., Esq., St. Leonard's, Killiney, co. Dublin.
Payne, George, Esq., J.P., Badwell Ash, Ixworth.
Priest, Mr., The Glebe, Methwold.
Procter, Rev. F., Witton Vicarage, North Walsham.
Ray, Rev. Henry, 22, Unthank's Road, Norwich.
Read, O. F., Esq., Mildenhall.
Rivers, Lieut.-Gen. Pitt, D.C.L., F.R.S., F.S.A.
Rye, Walter, Esq., Frognal House, Hampstead, N.W.
Thornton, H. K., Esq., Craigmellar, Victoria Road, Horwich, Bolton.
Todd, Mr. J. T., 9, Chapel Field Gardens, Norwich.
Upcher, H. M., Esq., East Hall, Feltwell, Brandon.
Valentine, J. S., Esq., 8, Campden House, Kensington.
Walsingham, The Rt. Hon. Lord, Merton Hall.
Whitta, Albert, Esq., Methwold.
Williams, C., Esq., F.R.C.S., 48, Prince of Wales' Road, Norwich.

CONTENTS.

	PAGE
CHAPTER I.—In British Times	1
„ II.—In Roman Days	15
„ III.—The Days of Pagan Incomers	21
„ IV.—In Norman Days	32
„ V.—In Plantagenet Days	38
„ VI.—In Tudor Times	58
„ VII.—In Stuart Times	79
„ VIII.—At the beginning of our Century	92
„ IX.—In my own Days	102

LIST OF ILLUSTRATIONS.

1.	Settlement Stone and Cross	*to face Dedication*
2.	Pre-historic Map of Methwold	*to face p.* 5
3.	British Settlement (conjectural)	,, 9
4.	Relics of Roman Farm Villa	,, 18
5.	Hall Farm, from Water Colour Sketch	,, 24
6.	Plan and part elevation of De Warennes' Residence	,, 32
7.	De Warennes' House in the Gloaming	,, 35
8.	Conjectural Restoration of Market Cross	,, 37
9.	View of Church, &c., from Ottering-hythe Road	,, 38
10.	Church Tower from the High Street	,, 42
11.	Interior of Church	,, 45
12.	Carving about Church	,, 46
13.	Rough Sketch of Church Roof	,, 48
14.	The De Clifton Brass	,, 51
15.	The Tudor Vicarage	,, 65
16.	Interior View and Woodwork of Vicarage	,, 67
17.	Tudor Bedstead	,, 69
18.	The De Mundeford Town House	,, 71
19.	A Tudor Gable recently demolished	,, 73
20.	Tudor Mantel and Hearth Curbs	,, 77
21.	Cradle of the Franck Family	,, 79
22.	Map of Methwold Parish	,, 82
23.	The Fair Hill	,, 102
24.	From the Fruit Colony by the Wents	,, 108

CHAPTER I.

𝔍𝔫 𝔅𝔯𝔦𝔱𝔦𝔰𝔥 𝔗𝔦𝔪𝔢𝔰.

ANYONE who in his later years has re-visited the home of his childhood, and gone over the ground once so familiar, after it has been dealt with differently by subsequent holders, who have built new constructions upon it, and altered its appearance here and there, finds a touching interest in recalling its old similitude, the presentment of the past that has remained indelible upon the more sensitive plates of childish memory, and comparing it with that before him. It is with something of this interest that one of the present century may take his stand near the churchyard of Methwold village; or town, as I believe it makes bold to style itself by right of a weekly market; and look down upon the green hollow below him which was the nest of the oldest settlement of humanity hereabouts, of which we can recover any traces; and endeavour to picture to himself what may then have been its appearance. He will begin by marking the watercourse, of which most of the bed is still traceable to the eye, though all that remains of the water is a narrow ditch from the left taking the drainage of the village street that slopes down beside us, and presently winds out of sight behind the houses; a duck pond in front of the Hall Farm opposite, 9 ft. deep still, by the way, in its centre, as was revealed when it was cleared out a few years since, one very dry summer; and a broader continuation of the drain thence to the right; dry, save in very wet seasons; which in old time met the Fen waters just where they crept in between the two rises opposite, and again, further on to the right, past the second rise.

The cause of the drying up of this water-bed, as also of certain square Norman fish-stews on the further side of it; now familiarly known as "the Sinks," because the water reappears in them occasionally in winter, only again to vanish,—we shall have to relate when we arrive at the fourteenth century of our era, and later yet, in Stuart times, when we speak of the history of the drainage of the Bedford level.

Why should one look first for the water-course? Because it is to that that the ground before him owes such slight definite formation as it possesses; and because he will remember that, in those early days to which he would return, the presence of water in a convenient form determined the locality of human settlements, for as yet the well-sinker was not; and, moreover, the streams formed the itinerary of the land,—by them men walked, by them men determined their whereabouts in a wild country overspread for the most part with furze, or copse, or forest.

It is only a poor sluggish stream that he recalls, a crawling rivulet that comes to him from the little valley which, to the left, separates the isolated chalk rise opposite from the general sweep of the mainland; and it is only separated by that rise from the great expanse of fen that stretches to the high island of Helingeye (Hilgay), and the lower isles of Modney (Moding-eye), and Southereye, seven or eight miles away. We catch the soft outline of the rich woods of Wood Hall, perhaps originally named from Wode or Woden, in Hilgay, through the break opposite.

Where this rivulet crossed the roadway, at the turn of the road to the hamlet which lay beyond the chalk rise, and which the Saxons re-named Ottering-hythe, as also in the leftmost bend of the grass land below him, he may discover that it once spread into a succession of pools—docks I fancy they were then called—for the form of many of them remains in the land; these the Romans called putei, and ever after they were called pits with a true rendering of the Latin pronunciation, nor are they quite gone yet from mention; for the corner of the road, where men splashed through them with naked shanks on the way to Ottering-hythe, that low corner where mists still rise as the ghosts of the departed waters; and where even water will be after a heavy downfall; is still named by men Pits-corner, or, alas! more usually Pitchcorner.

Let me remark here on a matter to which I shall often have occasion to refer. The conversion of names which have lost their significance into other names very like them which have still a significance, is one of the commonest corruptions of an earlier nomenclature.

As the Greek conquerors turned Jerusalem into Hierosolyma, and Kidron into Kedron; as Brum-mel, the broom-mound by Brandon, whose Priory received in Norman times the gift of the very ground beside those pits, became Broom-hill; so Pits-corner became Pitchcorner, because the pits were there no longer, but the pitch of the neighbouring rise was.

There are evidences of yet another pool or two in the course of the stream, besides that which alone survives as a duck pond; and from the other side of it were led dykes or fosses on either side of the quadrangular enclosure in which in Saxon times used to stand the house of the Earldoman; and where, perhaps, the big hut of the British chief had stood, and where the house known as the Hall Farm now stands.

It was but a slight stream, and the site is lowly. Wells enabled our later forefathers to be independent of the rivers and streamlets; and, in these days of waterworks, towns climb the loftiest suburbs; but then, for the needs of the home, for the convenience of the women, some natural reservoir must be had near the door of the hut; and there are villages where to this day similar needs are no better supplied. In this

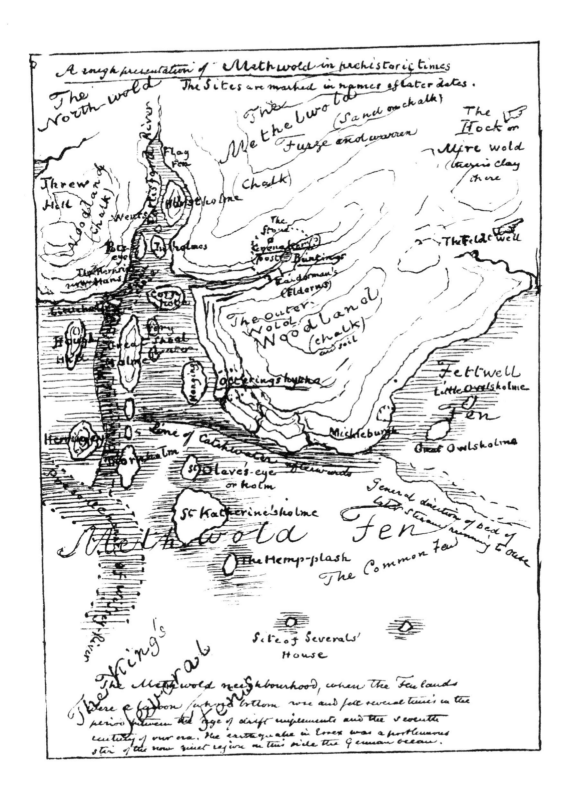

district, where the chalk absorbs rapidly the water that falls on a high-land frequently besprinkled with a sandy soil, water was then so rare and precious in the upland field that the one high-land spring hereabout could be called *par excellence* the "Felt Well," the spring in the veldt; and the spot where it gushed be sacred; so that, as often in the sister island, the church came to be built over it. And if this site be lowly, it was clear of the Fen, and yet conveniently near for purposes of fishing, and was one of those unmarked spots which gave a sense of retirement and security in the days when tribes were in constant warfare.

Here, then, our British forefathers set up a settlement on the banks of the streamlet, and marked their place with a stone, a sacred settlement-stone, precious to us as is London stone to the great metropolis, and this still is to be seen on the little triangular place where the roads diverge for the Ottering-hythe and for Feltwell, which has long been known as the Cross Hill. For, when the earliest missionaries of Christianity, perhaps even in British times, won a community to the new faith, they re-consecrated the old sacrificial stone, and dedicated it anew, by morticing a cross, if only a rough cross of timber, into it. Such stones, so treated, are still often to be observed—there is one at Feltwell—and deserve far more attention than is usually accorded them. Our settlement stone, since the days when, early in the present century, the road from Methwold to Mildenhall was first installed, had been gradually disappearing; and, when I came to the Parish, existed only in memory; but a few years since, a fortunate storm swept bare its upper surface; and I made haste to have it dug up and stored in a neighbouring garden, till it could be replaced above the present road level. There it was, a simple square of reddish freestone, very roughly tooled; moreover, the top of it to the depth of some inches had been altered to an octagon, in order that it might be bound with a ring of iron; for in the last century it had at last been split from corner to corner by the wedging in of a guide-post, where once the cross, and where later the May-pole may have stood. The smith had done his work well, and the stone bore safely its removal and replacement. Now it is placed within a yard of the original site, and a solid cross of oak erected in it, which is held firm by masonry and cement beneath, and a railed enclosure has been placed round it.

There are some who, not inexcusably, have called shame on me for the iron-work that rises from the top of the cross carrying a lamp for the service of humanity, and a pair of direction-boards for the convenience of the stranger. But we endeavoured to walk in the way of peace and charity; and all Christians have not the same way of looking at things: to some the bare cross was startling; so we combined with its most solemn aspect, other attributes of the Christ that should enter into common life, with the thought expressed in our Dedication.

Had our forefathers here not only a local habitation, but a name by which they knew it? Of course they had, but British nomenclature has for the most part been erased. Thus, whilst neighbouring Brandon is still pure Keltic, signifying perhaps the Brents' fort; for the fen near was Brents-fen, now translated Burnt-fen: the other Brandon (Branodunum) on the north coast is half Romanized into Brancaster. The Parish itself is full of Saxon and Scandinavian names, but not of Keltic. But it is barely possible that the name of the British village is still to be heard, in a personal name that hangs about the district and even the very locality. It may have been Greenacre or Grenaker, and have signified the Sun-fort.

The land adjoining the Cross Hill, on the last unoccupied portion of which the fine Parish Schools began to be reared thirty years ago by the Duchy of Lancaster, in whose hands the ground remained, was then called the Bone-close. For the meaning of this word Bone you must not think, as the neighbours naturally did, of burials, though part of the close across the road did early become a churchyard, for there, as we shall see later on, the church of the Saxon settlement was built; but you must think of bonfires, and Bonchurch, and perhaps, too, Mary-le-bone, not, I think, ever *la bonne;* of boon companions too, I believe, though often explained as *bons compagnons;* and remember that this word Bone, whatever its Keltic signification, is connected with the need-fires of Druidism. This probably was the early place of worship and ceremonial, not held under roof: and, in this connection, let me ask you to remember, that even the bodies of our mediæval churches, covered though they are, were regarded but as the courts of the Temple, so that men in the middle ages did not scruple to employ them for purposes not fully religious; and that they thus form a link with the half-sacred enclosures of British times, that had also their social uses. Let us suppose that the settlement was named Grenaker; that the Sun gave it its first syllable, as it has done to Grena, and Greenock, and Greenore, and Greenhythe, and Greenwich, where the Sun is still observed reverently.

As to the subsequent syllables, aker does not mean acre (ager), but must be compared with arx, citadel. It means whatever Arques does, where a castle near Dieppe, that once looked down on Henry IV. and the armies of his League before Ivry, stands on a Keltic mound. It means whatever Acra, the Domesday title for Castleacre and its surroundings meant. Now this root "ak," which exists abundantly, is Basque, probably the oldest tongue extant, and is found in axe, and acer, and acute, and perhaps in ache, signifies anything that has an edge; and Acra if it were a late Latin word, formed from *akron*, as burgh from *purgos*, correctly represents its force. But perhaps after all Castleacre was Grenaker before any castle was reared on it, and so we must leave our settlement nameless still. We may imagine our settlement, following the upper bend of the streamlet, to have had the form of

the letter S, and the stone to have marked the centre of the bend nearest us, the Bone Close lying just within it. Probably it was girt with a set, or fence, of close-grown thorn. The wold in which we stand guarded it from the east winds which have at all times affected the district, and even modified its speech. It was the east wind that made the Saxon North-folk sound Goodric as Goodrich, and Ethelric as Etheridge; it is the east wind that still makes the Norfolker, keeping down the centre of his upper lip, and speaking through the corners of the mouth, give that twang to his speech, which led a poor Norfolk lad amidst the thunders of the Redan to address General Wyndham in words, which were his very last utterance, "What! be yew tew fro Norfuk?" The opposite wold kept high away the flagging exhausting draughts from the vast lagoon of the Fens, and the southern sun lay warm in the hollow. So the site was not so undesirable after all. Circular huts, probably built of the clunch, the hard chalk, of which to this day houses and walls are mainly built, dotted either bank of the streamlet, amidst willow, alder, and indigenous poplar-growth, their cooking-stoves smoking outside. At summer time you may imagine women employed beside them in their rough cookery; or shaping their rude utensils of clay, marking them with lines of ornament by fish bones or their own long finger nails; or weaving baskets of the osiers, cut near; or scraping skins for clothing with thumb pieces of flint; or tailoring with knives of flint and awls of bone. The children are there, with the large white limbs the Romans noted, clamouring, and playing, and racing in and out of the pools, like the children of Palestine to-day.

Sometimes a man will come along the bank with fish strung on an osier, and his coracle hanging by the brow strap on his broad shoulders, which presently the boys will beg, and set afloat on the streamlet, squabbling for a turn at its use, and he will watch them, laughing as he leans on his pole spear, with its neat blade of flint turned upward for safety. Did he call it a "dag," I wonder? it is highly probable. If it be evening, we may see some youth striding down the slope opposite, a visitor from the settlement beyond it, watched for by some maiden in our possible Grenaker.

On some other day we might see a little company of the men returned from skirmishing with some neighbouring settlement, gashed and bruised, with perhaps, alas, a slave or two for the head man, or victims for the next Beltane, handing over axe in helve of wood, or bow of yew and sheaf of flint-headed arrows to the care of the women; and then stepping into the stream to wash, preparatory to the application of bruised leaves or roots by some hand to these rough ones accounted dear and tender.

And they had their Feast Days. In the latter part of our April came the spring feast of the Sun-God, a time of rejoicing to a people who had hardly the appliances of the Esquimaux for keeping themselves warm during the dreary winter. That day was alloted afterwards to St. George: naturally, too, if we trust those who say that the legend of this saint, originating as it did in the land of Adonis, is only a perverted form of the Sun-myth. And this is still the great feast day of Methwold, our *jour de l'an;* to St. George our church is dedicated; the principal hostelry bears his name; and the Annual Fair, for trade and sport, which yet inherits too much of the tone of paganism, so that whilst it lasts sins of revel are lightly accounted of, still comes on that day.

At that feast you might have seen the women baking on their cooking-stoves great store of flat cakes, marked with the sun's rays—we eat them still under the name of hot cross buns; and buns I suspect they called them, bone cakes or boon cakes that is, for bone is still sounded bun hereabouts. Perhaps boon companions shared one such cake between them, and kept his half to lie in his rude pillow, the sack that held his precious implements. And even then the feast was also a time for trade and barter; and the stone had its use for ratifying bargains, as the market cross was to have; and hands were clasped over it, and a natural libation squirted on them and on the stone.

There were robes of skin to be bought, and implements, some of them cut from minerals that no land nearer than Germany could produce. And at night the bonfire burned and crackled; and dancing went on round it; and love-making went hand in hand with religion, more conveniently then than under the bright light of Midsummer eve. Whether Grenaker laid its dead hereabout, or bore them to a slope across the water, a mile away to the right, where a diligent and adventurous colony of fruit growers has turned up quite a number of British burials, we cannot say. Perhaps that served only for another settlement, at the Gwent (now called the Vents or Wents), hard by the small stream of Pottisford, which divides Methwold from Northwold Parish. This stream takes its name from Pots-eye or Pot-eye, the pottery island, an island now no longer, though the name remains. Most of our fen parishes have their Pots-eye, or Pots-holms. It is not common to find a plot, as here, given up to Keltic burials, which are generally dotted singly, or gathered in small number round the door of some chieftain. The spot which we have referred to as the Vents (the name is also sounded, and more often in Norfolk written, Wynch) is marked now only by a single farm-house, but the peculiar formation of a couple of hundred yards of the road here, which lie across at right angles to the roads which enter at either end from Methwold and Northwold, and the indications of its having bordered a small watercourse in early days, probably give some guide to the extent of the settlement once to be found there.

CHAPTER II.

𝔍𝔫 𝔕𝔬𝔪𝔞𝔫 𝔇𝔞𝔶𝔰.

MANY local terms still in use in Norfolk point to the days when Britain had become a province of the great empire. In Norwich, a court or paltry square is still vulgarly called a loke (*locus*), the poles of the Norfolk wherryman are called quants, from contus, a late Latin word for a pole, taken like so many others of that date from the Greek. Already we have remarked the same of burgh, burgus, Greek *purgos*, and traced the use of the word pit for a pool to the Latin *puteus*.

Perhaps it was from the Latins that we learned here to call a boundary stream a string-dyke—Pottisford is so designated—from *stringere* to divide, or draw a line round; or again to know the boundary plantations towards Feltwell as the Tennis (*tenus*), unless we owe this to old Latin law terms of later date.

But we have in Methwold more tangible evidence of Roman possession. Their coins are frequently turned up here, as also in the neighbourhood of the Vents, especially on the fruit colony: perhaps they had provided Latinized Britons with the wherewithal for satisfying Charon. I have the head of a Bacchante draped in a fawn skin, done in terra cotta, that a trespassing urchin picked out of a chink in the cliff of the village chalk quarry: and to make their residence here more certain, I had the good fortune, in 1882, to assist in the partial unearthing of the remains of a Roman farm villa on the Fen border, some account of which, with the illustrations here reproduced, was published in the proceedings of the British Archæological Association, and noted by the *Times*.

Before describing these, I will say a word about the locality in which we found them. Where the watercourse talked of in my first chapter united itself with the Fen, beyond the second of the rises opposite, that which lies west of the right hand of one standing where I then placed the observer, lies now a dreary pool known as the Humble (Holme-brig) Pit; for just by here the causeway to various holmes in early mediæval times crossed the dwindling watercourse, which a drain cut from the above pit by one Hoggard or Haggard, and known as the Hoggard's-dyke, was presently to dry up altogether. From beside this pit starts a miry lane overhung by ash and alder, known as the Huns-road, from the Hern-lands or Heronries that it once led to. The neighbouring pastures are wet and swampy in winter: there willows flourish, and not long since a noted bat maker had his men employed for weeks in cutting out in the rough, bats to be wielded here or across seas by many a well-known hero of the cricket field. Thence are cut the alders and other light woods on which Lancashire experts, coming to lodge in the village, will labour for weeks, slicing them with something like a giant tobacco-cutter into the first rough semblance of clog soles. And, outmost of these wet lands, lies a field known as the Little-holme, rising very slightly to its centre, which was once, doubtless, an islet, and is often still pretty well awash in winter. None but a lunatic would now think of erecting a farm-house on such a site. Yet here this Roman farm-house was found.

The fact is that the Romans, in the matter of draining swamps, were more practical and common-sense engineers than we are yet. They succeeded in making this corner of our fen more habitable than it ever has been since. The plan they adopted here and elsewhere, and the one which recent writers allow to have been the only sensible one, was as follows.

They made a catch-water along the edge of the highlands, which occasionally, as here, took in a bay of the fen, sufficiently capacious to intercept and hold the high-land waters, and discharge them at either end into some considerable natural drain. Thus, left to deal only with its own rainfall, they found that much of the fen, the soil being light and porous, with the assistance of a few drainage cuts and its own small natural streams slightly deepened, was able to get rid of its own soakage.

We, following the plan which the Dutchmen initiated in the times of the Stuarts, have let their catch-waters fill up, and pump the high-land springs into and through the fens; rendering the total soakage, or "suck" as it is called, of the low lands our reservoir, and desiccating mischievously the border lands, to the detriment of the underlying flats. Every dweller in West Norfolk or Suffolk has marked this process of desiccation. A small stream that bore the name of the Linnett, from the Lynn-ait by Haberdon, whereon the inhabitants of Bury once fought their camp fights or legal duels—just as the Wensum is named from the Gwents-holme, now Thorpe islet—affords a notable instance. This, rising five miles away in the park at Ickworth, and flowing through a deep channel of its own delving by Westley and Horning's Heath, often marked 6 ft. in winter on the post by Stamford Bridge, where it crosses the road from the Westgate of Bury, half a century ago. Now, in company with a hundred other streams named or un-named in these border lands of Norfolk and Suffolk, it is often totally dry the whole year round. To take instances nearer at hand. We have already spoken of the drying up of the streams, such as they were, at Methwold and the Vents. At Feltwell, the street which winds to the west once bordered the brook that flowed from the well; and the bed of this still leads unaltered, though bone dry, through the grass lands beyond, and beside it lies an ancient moat, now so distant from all idea of water that the rustics account for its presence by abundant myths and conjectures. This stream was intersected and tapped lower down by the fen-dyke known as Dr. Sam's Cut, as we shall see in Stuart times, and has vanished from the high land. There is evidence that the main street of the next parish also, Wilton, once bordered a similar rivulet.

But there is another point of interest that concerns the locality of our Roman farm. On this side the Fen, as also on the Wisbech side, the Romans presented a line of low earthworks, surmounted with a palisade, alternating where convenient into the defence offered by some natural stream, as a sort of "Tenus" against the Fen-dwellers, who already were, probably, many of them "Saxons" of some kind.

Here this vallum, later named the Grimsdyke (compare Grimshoe, the name of the hundred, and Grimes Graves, the flint workings examined by Canon Greenwell at Weeting) ran at the extreme limit of our parish to the south, nearly two miles back of Littleholme. Starting from the Little Ouse near Brandon Ferry, it ran as far as the Wissey stream at Cranwich (Crane-vic), and, after being replaced by the Wissey and its tributary that borders Boughton-fen as far as Bechamwell, passes thence to the Nar below Castleacre, and is once more replaced by that stream as far as Lynn haven. Brandon, Ickburgh (*Icenorum burgus*), and Oxburgh, the water-fort, with Narburgh and perhaps Acra by Nar, guarded it to the east. Hence this Roman farm was outside the line, and must have been the possession of some adventurous Roman colonist who took his chance without the vallum on the recently drained lands.

But the finding of urns packed with coins, probably a portion of some military chest "cached" in retreat, some years since in Feltwell, also shows that the Romans after a time made incursions beyond their own lines. There is reason to think that this one farmer suffered for his adventurous spirit, and that his farm was burnt down by the fenmen.

For years tiles had been turned up by the plough on Little-holme, during attempts to render it arable, which have been now abandoned; and those who noticed them supposed them to be the outcome of some forgotten brick-kiln. But at last the foundations were touched, and large pieces of ashlar of fine-grained grey Northampton stone began to make their appearance. They could only have been brought here by water, which is another proof of Roman activity. An examination of the spot was determined on, and the illustration shews with what result. On a solid foundation of ashlar with bands of flint-work, a structure apparently of timber, for wood-ash abounded, had been reared, sufficiently solid to bear a roof of heavy red tiles of an excellent design; and it must have been a

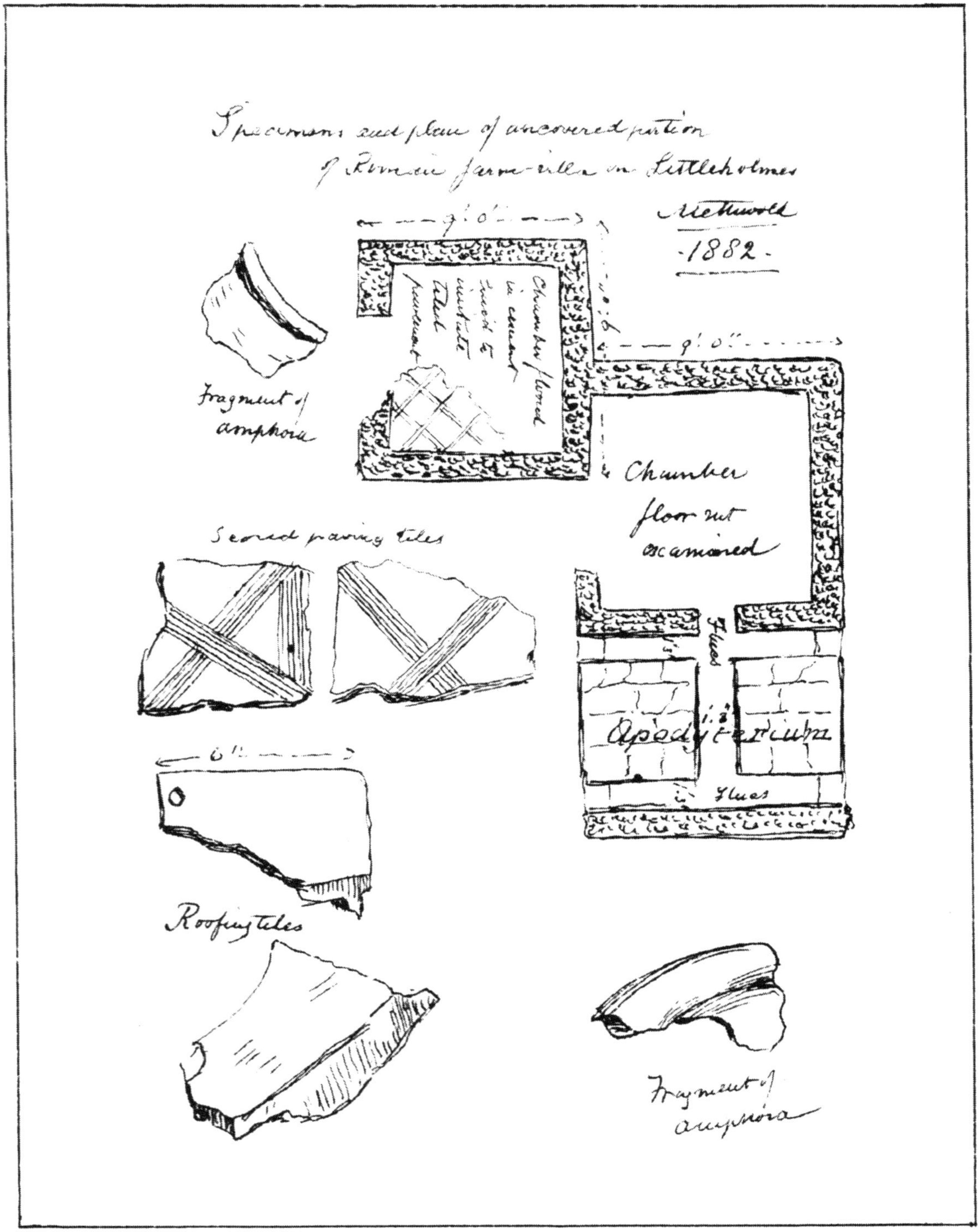

Specimens and plan of uncovered portion of Roman farm-villa in Littleholmes

Methwold
1882

Fragment of amphora

Scored paving tiles

Roofing tiles

Chamber floor not examined

Apodyterium

Flues

Fragment of amphora

respectable residence, for it possessed a small apodyterium with a floor of solid concrete, intersected by flues. Three only of the apartments, probably thalami (sleeping-chambers), were uncovered, of which one was floored with tiles with an incised pattern, whilst another had been laid with cement, lined to simulate tiles. So the Romans had penetrated into our community with their architecture and agriculture, and doubtless also their horticulture, and their social culture also; and their British neighbours had learned of them good as well as evil; education, and manners, and dress, as well as vices and amusements; and the youth of the settlement would have to compete with them in style and civilization, if they did not wish to be cut out by the new-comers in the favor of those white-armed maidens to whom the Romans took so kindly.

Some of the legionaries, and these were of most divergent nationality, may have brought Christianity under their notice, if they did not already find it here; and thus stronger than mortal ties may have made them of one family with their British neighbours. British Christianity existed, and was of a purer type than that finally established amongst the Saxons; and British civilization had reached a higher level before the departure of the Romans than it regained before the present century. When we think of the roads that some of our forefathers here must have seen and traversed in the fourth century, and remember that till the present century nothing worthy of the name of a road existed between us and the neighbouring villages as far as Mildenhall, we mentally picture Methwold in Roman times as having made an astonishingly rapid advance upon its mental and material condition in the former chapter.

CHAPTER III.

The Days of Pagan Incomers.

I CANNOT say when these days began; when first Frisian and Scandinavian, and all that went under the generic name of Saxon, began to drift in at the wide mouth of the Wash, and take up their abode in the Fen or on its borders. Kemble may well be right in his conjecture that they even preceded the Roman settlement, and that much of the *Saxonicum littus* was a *Saxonia Propria*.

It is curious that there is no clear evidence of a warlike subjection of these counties when the Saxons and Angles were possessing themselves of other parts of Britain. It seems rather as if they had drifted more quietly over the land through openings long secured, and amidst a population more or less inured to their presence. How, but on the supposition of their presence in considerable numbers, can we account for the well-supported tradition that in the fourth century a prefect of Branodunum (Brancaster) calculated on making a successful pronunciamento by their aid? When, too, did many of the Fen islets first take Scandinavian names? One at least I know in Mildenhall must have been called a holme, before the use of the word "eye" was customary for an islet, for now it is called Holms-eye. And the later incursions of the Danes never extended over many grounds that yet, at some time, had acquired Scandinavian names. The holmes and hocks in the Fen are past all counting. When the Danes came in armies, they despised such poor localities, and made for the better lands. Nowhere hereabouts do we find their "bys." The nearest is Risby, inland of Bury St. Edmund's.

Holmes lie all along the fiord or arm of the Fen here known as Pottisford, which in Roman times ceased to be islands or anything like it. Such are Harst-holme, corrupted into Harvest-holme, on the way to Cranwich; In-holme between the Vicarage and Potseye; Corn-holme by the Hall Farm, the "second rise" of the first chapter; Little-holme, Great-holmes, and the holmes generally beside which Pottisford makes its way to the Wissey. Sleves-holme and Kats-holme, dedicated to the Scandinavian Saints St. Olave (or Olaf) and St. Catherine, lie further out; and may, again, have been islands at a later date, when they were chosen for Sanctuaries.

Here let me note that the degeneration of holme into ham is very common. Thus Dere-holme (the game islet) became Dereham; Were-holme (the inhabited islet), Wereham; Ford-holme, by Snorr and Hilgay, Fordham; and St. Olave's-holme and Kat's-holme have become at last in the rustic speech Slusham and Catsham.

But, however early Teutons of some sort may have found their way into this neighbourhood, it must have been after the Angles were fairly settled on the land, that the chalk rise, on which the observer was invited to take his stand in our first chapter, received its name of Methelwold (Mittelwald, Middlewold), which is now shortened into Methwold; and that the sept of the Buntings occupied and gave their name to the settlement in the hollow; whilst that of the Otterings similarly occupied Ottering-hythe, over the opposite rise and on the edge of the Fen. The Buntings must have meant the people of the Grey or Grizzled one—the Grays, in short; the Otterings, if Otter be Angle for Oder, as probably it is, the Blacks; Scottice the Douglases. Anyhow, the village is no longer nameless, and this name of Buntings still to this day clings to the lowest part of the village. Let us try to realize this East Anglian village of Buntings as the Normans found it.

It still lies in the hollow; but the circular huts have now given place to rude rectangular cottages, and there are a few timber edifices of much the same pattern, but on a larger scale, for the heads of the community. Chief among these latter, across the water, where we supposed the hut of the British chief might have stood, is the house of the Ealderman on the site of the Hall Farm; for the lane which leads to this from Pits Corner is still, with but slight compaction of the syllables, called the Eldern's Lane. It stood facing nearly east, on a levelled and defended platform, with dykes from the rivulet of which the depressions remain on either side. Probably there were palisades on the inner edge of the dykes; and it looks as if there had been a porter's lodge on a small artificial island; for the line of its square moat remains; at the head, I suppose, of the bridge by which its enclosure was approached.

The site has never since been unoccupied. When the De Warennes built, as we shall see, in Norman times, their residence on the opposite slope of the Methelwold, they probably made a home-farm of the Ealderman's house; and the Hall Farm, some parts of which may have a very early date, is there now. Opposite this, but more to our left as we look down from Methwold, is the rectangular field, also dyked round, on which, as we have said, after Christianity had been first encouraged and then virtually enforced by royal patronage, arose the first church, the church of Buntings. Of this fact, suspected by me from the first, as the enclosure belonged early to the Priory at Brummel, which had the patronage of the living, and their tithe barn still stands on its southern edge, there is no longer a shadow of doubt: for when, some

Cottage from a sketch of the Nott House in 1868 (now the Parsonage) (Eldemus / heirs?) done by the wife of a Wesleyan Dean for 1868.

years ago, a wretched farm-house of Stuart date, framed in rough oak and filled in with clunch and mud-like mortar, was pulled down to give place to a pair of cottage villas, the entire foundation of the chancel, a mass of rough concrete 3 ft. thick, was uncovered; and with their help, and the evidence of the position and width of the west end, traceable beyond some intervening outbuildings in the neighbouring enclosure referred to above, the plan of a simple nave slightly wider than the chancel was easily recovered, and it at once became plain that a small position of wall in rubble and flint which stood at right angles to the first of these outbuildings, and which it was declared no pick could disintegrate and remove—alas! it is cleared away now—was actually a portion of the south wall of the nave.

From beside the foundations of the chancel I recovered a couple of octagonal drums of a small pillar,* precisely matching another that had long been lying about on neighbouring premises, and also a

---

* During the demolition, early in the present year, of some late Tudor work in brick and flint diapered, that still formed the front of a portion of an old farm-house, long since divided into cottages, on the east side of the Fair Hill, the drum of an octagonal column was discovered, which corresponds in character with the smaller columns, one of which has been employed as a pilaster for the basin of the piscina to the guild chapel at the east end of the north aisle of the present church; whilst others, now lying by the settlement-stone, were discovered amongst the foundations of the earlier church by Buntings. It is probable, therefore, that this drum is a portion of a column of the arcade of the earlier church, and proves that it was in the possession of at least one aisle at the time of its replacement by the present Decorated church on the brow of the Methel-wold.

similar pillar which had been preserved and converted to a singular use in the present church.

This last, supplied with a rough base and a moulded capital, in different stone and of Perpendicular date, has been made to serve as a piscina, probably to the altar of a Guild Chapel, in the north aisle. What purpose these small columns can have served in the original church is difficult to determine.

The first church here would probably have been of timber, as that still standing at Grenstead (the hedge or enclosure of the sun) in Essex; the flint and stone edifice, if we may judge from these traces, would not date from before the Conquest. This must have been the Parish Church of Buntings, and of Methelwold, until the later church, just east of the Hall Close, was built after the extinction of the line of the De Warennes, on what was probably till the reign of Richard II. part of the Fair Ground or Market.

A third moated enclosure, made up like that on which the church stood to a level rectangular platform, existed and exists on this same side of the stream a few hundred yards to our right. This held probably a thane's residence. Somewhere, probably where the school now stands, the chaplain would have his residence, not in those days wanting its female denizen in the shape of wife, or, as the stricter Churchmen termed such, concubine; or dull for the lack of childish voices; for the complete celibacy of the clergy, though aimed at from the time of Dunstan, was but very slowly secured in England, where to this extent the Saxon clergy followed the habits of their British forerunners at the first. I think the road even from British times followed the lines of the present street, for at the edge of the wold it is ground deep into the soil, like the hollow-ways of Belgium, so that the churchyard on the one side and the garden attached to an old Tudor house recently demolished,* on the other, have a level higher by some 3 ft. or so at least than that even of the present street.

Ottering-hythe also had its church, now entirely disappeared and ploughed up even to the foundations, which equally serves to localize the earliest settlement there, for the Church Piece still retains its title, and the patronage of it gave occasion to long-lived disputes in Plantagenet times, between Brummel Priory, which laid claim to it as part of the patronage of Methwold, and the De Warennes, lords of the soil, within the limits of whose land, now vested in the Duchy of Lancaster, the oblong excrescence of the Church Piece is now included, they having made good their claim. By this time, too, the cells attached subsequently to the Priory of Castleacre must have been established on the holmes of St. Olave and St. Katherine. The lands of the latter, up to a very recent period, paid a modus to the Earls of Leicester. It will be remembered that, after Evesham fight, the

---

* See illustration given, "In Tudor Times."

property of Simon de Montfort was given to Edmund, Earl of Lancaster, second son of Henry III.; but this small possession may have been overlooked, since it is so long found in connection with the earlier title. From the highest ground on the former, two stone coffins were removed within the present century, which, after long filling the office of horse troughs on a farm at Ottering-hythe, have now entirely disappeared. By hints of their form and appearance, obtained from some of the oldest inhabitants, I fancy they must have dated from the eleventh or the twelfth century. Perhaps by this time the wooden cross on the settlement-stone had been replaced by one of stone. Probably the festivities on the Bone Close were still carried on in a modified form, and kept alive many superstitions, for Paganism is very hard to slay; sacred stones and other relics of Paganism are still precious and held serviceable in Scotland, and as we shall see in the end, superstitions that have come down from the earliest times are still treasured in Methwold. The religion of a departed race furnishes the superstitions of its successors in all lands. The sacred stone of eld still gives sanctity to the Mosque at Mecca; the Romans took their superstitions from the vanishing Etruscans; the Firbolgs of Ireland were the demi-gods and fairies of their Keltic successors.

One needs not to recall here the habits of Saxon life, they have been so abundantly described and illustrated elsewhere. Slight, too, as are the traces of their presence which they have left on the soil of Methwold or Buntings, they are rather more distinct than in most places; for the Saxons never threw up heavy earthworks, like the Britons, being little addicted to archery; and preferred the close fight on open ground, or utilized the fen and woodland for ambush and surprise. No race has left less mark on the soil which they have occupied, because none has depended more on personal prowess, or held fortifications in equal contempt.

I am aware, whilst I pen this, that a recent heresy has sprung up, which has, I fancy, had its birth in Norfolk; and that mounds like that at Norwich are attributed to the Romans; whilst that at Castleacre, to which possibly the Romans added the quadrangular extension, which served for the later ballium, as more suited to their formation, has been credited with a Roman and even with a Saxon origin; but of what earthly use to a Roman legion would a citadel, just suited to a tumultuous body of Keltic archers and axe throwers, have been? And what a hindrance would they have found in its irregular heaps of outwork. One has only to read Tacitus, and see how through Pannonia they scorned even to utilize the fortresses it took a lengthy circumvallation to clear of their tenants, to understand how contrary to the genius of Roman warfare is such a supposition. The Romans needed more ground for their formation than these Keltic mounds afford: only when they found a considerable enclosure, on the flat, as at Caistor, could they make it serve the same purpose as their castellum at Burgh. And when writers talk of Saxon "burhs," one would ask where in Kent, where by Anderida, where in Wessex, they resorted to such defences? Had such existed, Alfred would hardly have needed to find a natural refuge in Athelney; or have failed, when he had once more collected sufficient forces for a fight in the open, to take care to provide himself with such defences afterwards. But the fact is there was no such narrow tribal cohesion amongst the Saxons, as would have rendered the erection of such works practicable; their aim from the first was, not localities, but large districts: they never thought of stopping only where they were, but of spreading forward. Always thinking of attack, so long as there was anything to attack,—they were singularly reckless in their defensive arrangements. Had it been otherwise, the Normans would have been as long in conquering England as the Romans were; but, beyond such natural fastnesses as the Fens afforded, there was nothing then to oppose the complete overrunning of the country except armies in the field; and, once in, the Normans took care to erect the castles which the Saxons had been without. Ireland offers evidence that the Scandinavian branch of Teutons (the Danes) did erect earthworks; but, if one follows up their line from Waterford to Limerick, and compares their earthworks with those of the Kelts, which exist in numbers, one at once marks the fact that they differ from these latter in having always a set pattern, consisting of a platform with a "cavalier" raised at one end, and never taking the irregular form of a scarped mound, with outer mounds thrown up just anywhere and anyhow, as at Thetford, or Castleacre, or Castle Rising, and everywhere in Ireland.

CHAPTER IV.

In Norman Days.

OF all the many estates granted by the Conqueror to his sister's husband, Earl de Warenne, none seems to have more taken his affection than the Manor of Methwold. Perhaps he saw in the warrens—with which so much of the high land here was then occupied—a certain fitness, and a reminder of the lands on the other side of La Manche, which gave him his name. So celebrated were the warrens of Methwold even down to the present century, that the title of "Muel" rabbits was affixed to most rabbits offered for sale in London, just as most oysters were long put forth as Colchester natives; and as geese, though bred round Ostend, still somehow claim to be of Norfolk. Anyhow, the residence which the Earl reared on the slope of the Methelwold, facing towards the ealderman's abode from the rise on this side the stream,

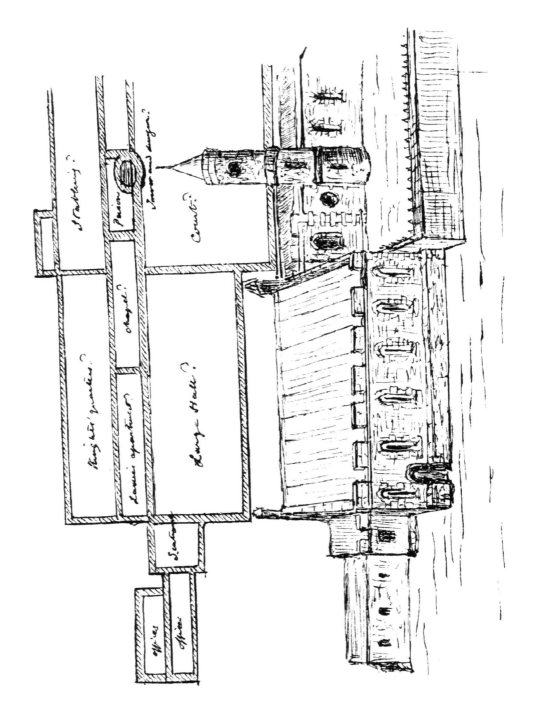

was apparently the headquarters of the family to the last, so that the last paper signed with the signature of the last childless descendant of the Great Earl, in the time of Edward I., shortly before the lands of the family passed, on his decease, into the hands of Edmund, Duke of Lancaster, second son of the royal vacillator, to become from the time of Henry IV. a personal possession of the Sovereign, is dated from "Methelwold." But from the incoming here of the Normans, the place bore yet another name. So thoroughly had these descendants of hoarse-throated rovers framed themselves by this time to the utterance of that rippling babble of low Latin which is now styled French, that the straggling name of Methelwold, with its heavy finial and its medial aspirate, was altogether unacceptable, and was softened down to Muelle or Muel; just as Antwerp has been Gallicized into Anvers, or Muhlhaüsen into Melouse. And this name held its place in common parlance up to the last half century, though it has pretty well fallen into disuse in these days of education and railway porters. But to this hour the Fen men call a north-easter a "Muel wind," because, straight in the eye of it, backed by the harmonious grays of a chilly horizon, rises, on a marked knoll, the tower of Methwold with its octagon and spire.

I say the great Earl made this his headquarters, but he was buried, nearer the Channel and his older home, at the priory which he founded where Southern Ouse creeps by the green mounds of

Lewes; and the two leaden coffins, that contained respectively his mortal remains and those of his princess consort, marked with their initials cut out of the same metal, were actually come upon during the construction of the London and Brighton Railway. One may wonder that he was not content to be laid in the grounds of the priory which he had founded at Castleacre (Acra) fourteen miles away from Methwold, but perhaps some sense of greater nearness to Normandy and to the royal town of Winchester may have influenced the imagination of his wife, who preceded him to the grave, in her choice of her place of sepulture.

The foundations of the De Warennes' residence extend through two-thirds of the width of this grass piece, which is called the Hall Close, or sometimes, by children, the Duchy Meadow. The outer bailey was apparently to the east of the Castle or residence: a considerable portion of it was some years since taken into the churchyard. The inner bailey occupied the space between it and the watercourse, which seems to have been dammed across, so as to render it of more respectable dimensions. The wall of the present churchyard is coped with the coping-stones of the castle enclosure, which are deeply grooved at the top, for the insertion of a palisade of iron or spiked timber.

Standing on the platform of the tower of the present church which surrounds the octagon, when the level rays of the westering summer sun swept the sward of the close, so as to adopt the device by

which so many of the sites of cities that once dotted the Roman Campagna have been recovered, I was able, some years since, to trace out something of the lines of the foundations of the departed residence, whose stones still served, some of them at least, as late as Tudor times, to chequer the gable of the town house of the De Mundeford's hard by, whilst the larger portion of them were probably utilized in the erection of the present church. It is evident that upon the dying out of the De Warennes, and the lapsing of the property into royal hands, the castle was either intentionally demolished, or, not impossibly, the materials were granted for the building of the church—or fell into rapid decay; which would not be a slow process, as we may gather, from what remains of the walls above the surface, that they were constructed of the clunch of the locality, which rapidly chalders if once deprived of its coping and casing. At the spot marked for a tower in the plan, a notable depression in the soil gives sinister hint of a possible oubliette; if so, the adjoining apartment would have been the chamber of examination and torture. With regard to the imaginary reproduction of the buildings of the residence given here and at the commencement of the chapter, we need hardly say that they are not the work of an adept, but they may serve as aids to the imagination of the past.

Between the outer and inner bailey are two lines of terrace—here possibly may have been fruit gardens—

whilst on the opposite side of the stream are the square fish-ponds which we have already spoken of as the Sinks, which in winter still occasionally provide convenient skating rinks for the village lads. Into the northmost of these, such drainage from the Fair Hill as passed on the north side of the enclosure, was conducted through a small catchpool or clearance basin, whose arrangements are still discernible. It was just to the south of this that a dam was thrown up, which, however well it may have served its purpose by spreading the stream for awhile as a defence, could not but ensure the rapid silting up of the bed of the watercourse.

With the building of the De Warenne's residence on this slope, and the change of the name of the village, must have come a tendency to remove the houses of the inhabitants out of the hollow; indeed, the widening of the stream would have rendered many of the original sites untenable; but it is plain, from a cursory survey of the village, that up to Tudor times it extended but little to the east of the present churchyard and the Fair Hill; and that the eastern half of the High Street has grown up since the days when anything of beauty clung to domestic architecture.

Probably with the settlement here of the De Warennes, the Spring Fair increased in importance, and it is conjectured that it became known as a peltry*

---

* The fur trade, now removed to Brandon, was carried on here still within the present century.

market, and flourished on that trade in rabbit skins of which Thetford and Brandon have since become the centres. Just east of the bailey wall lay a spot of rough ground, part of which is now the churchyard. To this ground the market was probably removed from the neighbourhood of the Cross Hill, which was now built upon; for there still stands here, within the churchyard, the rubble base of an octagonal cross, probably the original market cross, which, by its character, must have been of older date than the church. Whether the fragment recovered in digging a grave at its foot can anyhow be so pieced in as to give a notion of the original cross, as in the illustration, or whether the palm branch decoration shows it to have been part of an early tombstone, is left to the judgment of the reader.

We make no conjectures as to the history and condition of Methwold during this period, as it ought to be attested by documents which must surely exist in the keeping of the authorities of the Duchy of Lancaster, which we hope some one yet may care to produce. Application on my part to the office, in the earlier years of my incumbency, failed to draw out any information, or any hint that it would be accessible to an outside enquirer.

CHAPTER V.

In Plantagenet Days.

AS our notes on the Norman period are mainly concerned with the home of the De Warennes, so those that deal with the period lying between the third Henry and the seventh of that name must be most concerned with the church which is still the chief ornament of Methwold. It must have been somewhere in the reign of the unfortunate son of the Black Prince, and during the Florid or Decorated period of Gothic architecture, whose extravagance of beauty was very short-lived, that first a church was reared on that corner of the Fair Ground which projected behind the south-east corner of the Hall Close, and which probably had served for the regular market for some centuries. Had the church been built here a century or two earlier, the market might still have been held on the old spot; for it was only in the reign of Edward III. that an edict was issued for the

removal of fairs and markets from churchyards to some neighbouring ground. The long use of the body of St. Paul's in London as a place of exchange, and for business interviews, was but a survival in a solitary instance of immemorial habit that dated from pre-Christian times. Something of the same ancient feeling that religion and business were connected, which so long made the churchyards the place of trade, and has made markets in towns to locate themselves by the Cathedral or the principal church in such numberless instances, and which took men to the Market Cross, as earlier to the settlement-stone, for the ratifying of bargains, still affected the social business of the parish, and the parish meetings of one sort or another, for centuries after trade had been banished from the precincts. And we still retain the idea, though we may not perceive it, in our vestry meetings. Earlier they were held, and that down to Reformation times, not in the vestry, but in the body of the church, then regarded only as the outer court of the sanctuary, or sanctuaries. It was this manner of regarding the "pillared court" that long—not unwholesomely—affected the character of the sermon as there delivered, and made it a healthy link between worship and actual out-door life; we recognize this tone still in the sermons of Latimer and others, delivered at Paul's Cross. Now that the sermon has become an integral part of a differently-regarded worship, and has been, at least until lately, regarded as the most important part of "Divine Service," it is impossible, safely, to recover that old feeling with regard to the body of our churches, which was not altogether mistaken, and which tended to prevent too abrupt a division of Christian life into things sacred and things secular, the cutting off of the church and the Sunday from business and week-day.*

But the churchyard here could no longer have been suffered to be used for trading purposes at the date when this church was fully built. The Fair Hill, which lies to the north of it, must alone have afforded space for the ordinary market and the Fairs henceforward.

Of the original Decorated church only the chancel and the chancel arch, and possibly the tower, without the octagon and spire, remain; and these do not remain unmodified, for the side walls of the chancel and the ground floor of the tower have been furnished with Perpendicular windows, and the east window of the chancel alone displays the original tracery.

One of those traditions, guaranteed by no written

---

* Churches seem to have been utilized also, even for some time after the Reformation, for religious and for musical instruction. To some extent the Sunday School system replaced a lost habit. At the present day, in Catholic countries, where there is only secular instruction in the schools, there is daily catechizing by the village priest in the nave of the church before breakfast, and in the pre-Reformation period in England, catechizing was probably daily conducted in the same pleasant and familar manner. It is to be questioned whether religious instruction by the clergyman in the village schools, with secular surroundings, and within sound of the cane, can ever be productive of quite so good effect; and it may be that the declension of manners amongst the lower classes, which had reached its worst at the early part of the Georgian era, may have had its origin, to some extent, in the cessation of this wholesome contact between the impressible young and the clergyman of the parish.

record, but handed down from generation to generation of the inhabitants, which may generally be accepted as veracious, tells that the body of the original church was destroyed by fire within a century of the time of its erection. The free use of unguarded candles in Romish ceremonies always rendered such conflagrations frequent; we have hardly a cathedral that has not suffered at some time in this way; Ely had so suffered but shortly before this church was erected. By whose liberality the church was built, and so far re-built, I have had no means of learning; but, as I have before said, the early disappearance of the residence hard by, and the use of the coping-stones of its walls for the walls of the churchyard, renders it probable that for its erection we may be indebted to the Dukes of Lancaster, and that they granted the material of the disused residence towards it.

But, when the present nave with its enlarged aisles—for the east walls of the smaller Decorated aisles are embodied in the present ones—was built a century later, perhaps the affection of the parish for the Lancastrians was hardly so thorough as might have been expected.

I have said that it looks as if the erection of the tower had preceded the fire; for although the great western window is Perpendicular, and marked, as it is, by the three crosses introduced into the stone-work of its tracery, is the counterpart of the west window at Fincham; and though the stone octagon and crocketted spire are also unquestionably of

G

Perpendicular date, still the lights of the bell-chamber have a Decorated character, and the filling up of the angles of the upper masonry of the tower within by brickwork, by which its covering is converted into a vault with a well mouth, on the lip of which the octagon and spire rest, has all the appearance of a subsequent insertion.*

The design of the tower, with its superstructures as they now appear, is, I fancy, unique in England. The belfry of Bruges, celebrated by Longfellow, when the spire—which was of lead and timber, and perished by fire—remained, must have presented a very similar combination, and perhaps have suggested the design here: it is not impossibly a work of the same architect in more durable material. Probably the tower itself had been completed only shortly before the fire; and was modified by the insertion of the large west window and the addition of the octagon and spire in stone, when the new nave and aisles had been completed, the abundance of stone from the castle affording materials to suggest so ambitious a use of them.

Out of my susceptibility to my surroundings for a score of years past, I seem to feel that the church carries a record of matters in the past which have had their effect in forming the present character of

---

* Also, had the octagon and spire been part of the original design, they would have been prepared for, and built on the actual centre; instead of which they are placed a foot back of the centre, so as to accommodate themselves to the thrust of the tower buttresses.

the community, which I will here endeavour to evolve. For Methwold is a community with a distinctive character of its own, that renders it an appreciable and affectionable entity, and one is naturally interested to discover how its individuality has been formed. It is of a very independent spirit, and has no awe of wealth and greatness such as usually characterizes our eastern villages. No one here, not even the most impressionable, would speak with bated breath even of the Queen; but it has a respect of its own, or perhaps rather an affection, for those who use a superior position well, especially if they be in any way connected with itself; though it in no case waives the right of free criticism. To outsiders, foreigners as they call them, it is cold and suspicious. I think the history of the past may explain this. It had known at an early date, in the case of the De Warennes,* grandees of the first magnitude, partly royal, for indwellers; and, possibly from something in the disposition of members of that house, I fancy that good family relations had arisen between

---

* Perhaps it may serve to put our readers in touch here with contemporary history, if we remind them that it was the home-coming of Earl Warenne, the great upholder of Edward I.'s early "unionism" in Scotland, on account of his now fast-failing health, and the handing over of the management to Cressingham, who took his title from a neighbouring parish, that led to the battle of Cambuskenneth, fought by Wallace for "Home-rule," which, in the ordering of Providence, led through subsequent events to a re-separation of the kingdoms for several centuries. How vain are the efforts to put on the clock of time! How true it is that what comes by the sword perishes by the sword, sooner or later, or has always to be so maintained.

the castle and the community, that a mutual tie of respect and affection existed, sufficient to overcome all disadvantages of scenery and climate, and make the Earl's family content to sign themselves as of Methwold to the last. Many traces exist in various localities of such humanizing connection between lord and peasant in Norman and Plantagenet days. If it were so, the breaking of all such ties by the passing away of the tenure of the lands to royalties who were necessarily strangers, the sight of the demolition of the residence, and the general sense of desertion, would have produced a feeling which the absenteeism of the gentry has within the present century made familiar to many of us in the country. The impersonal Duchy of Lancaster has always been suspiciously regarded in Methwold. And this feeling of distance from the superior classes has been since enhanced, by the alienation and dispersal amongst many owners of the Great Tithe, and the general non-residence of the possessors of land in the parish.

No one who has known Methwold need cross the St. George's Channel to study the mischievous effect of absenteeism. One of the representatives of the Duchy, a Surveyor-general, a genial and very human personage—recently, alas! deceased in his prime—by visits more frequent and prolonged than ever had been made by his predecessors, won a great amount of personal affection here in his time; and Methwold quite took him to its heart, as if he had filled an instinctive want. Alas! he was a man of ideas and

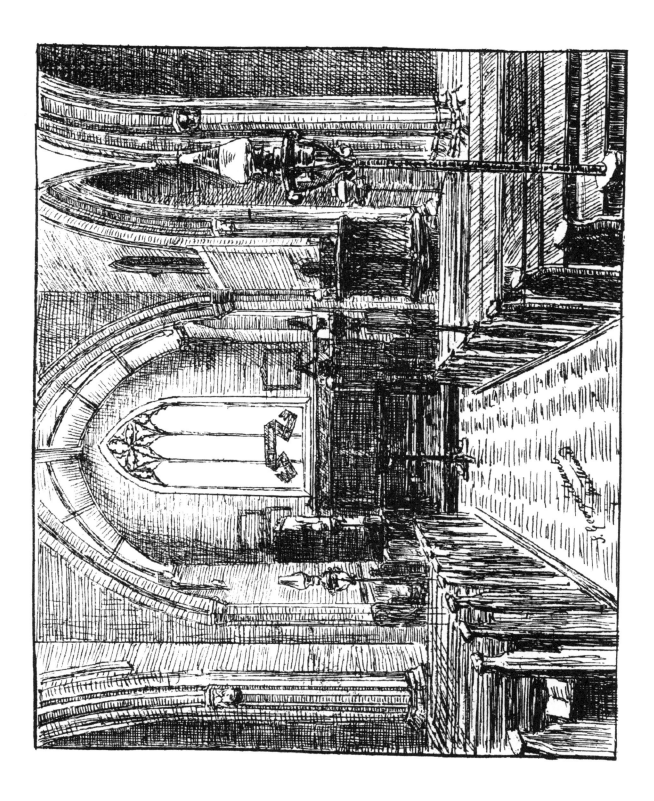

intentions for good, which, synchronizing unluckily with the setting in of the long period of agricultural depression that has prostrated the parish; and misguided, thanks to a designing adviser from the northern possessions of the Duchy, failed of profit in the execution; so we fear the very name of Methwold became an illness to him; and so the prospect of establishing a tangible and pleasant connection with the Duchy, through him, was more than disappointed.

Now I have a notion that we shall find, even in the church fabric, signs of this growing chill between Methwold and its now royal owners. Kings were at best impersonal; and, about that time, even the right of the sovereignty, and, with it, of the possession of Methwold manor, was a bone of contention; and I think we may point to an evidence that sneers flung at one or the other of its claimants or their families were not unwelcome in Methwold.

The evidence to which I refer is writ in stone, as will be presently indicated.

Observation of the various carved works about the interior of the church seems to prove that their execution was committed to two carvers of different temperament, the one more purely conventional and ecclesiastic in tendency, no bad workman, but possessed of slight individuality; the other, to whom the work of many of the capitals fell, a free-lance, something of an *ésprit fort*, and possessed of a vein of mockery; such a one as would tickle his rustic convives over their cups at the Crown, hard by the gates of the Hall Close, with suggestions risky to their loyalty, and suggestive of daring criticism on authorities; and leave a memorial of his individuality behind for them in his work. To him, we think, may have been entrusted the exterior adornment of the clerestory; for, carven with the assiduity of enjoyment, on the corbels of the central clerestory window in the south wall, looking full on the High Street, we see, on the one side a clever mocquante feminine head, with its coif of the time of Henry VI. and Edward IV., caught back to let the face leer askance towards the sorry display on the rival corbel, where a noble bearded male head lies exposed on a circular charger. Ecclesiastically, of course, we have Herodias and the Baptist's head; politically, Margaret, she-wolf of France, I fancy, and the head of the good Duke of Gloucester, recently done to death in his chamber by the northern postern of Bury Abbey. Other corbels on the same wall convey jokes, usual enough, at the coiffures of the period; perhaps one may be a caricature of the lovely goldsmith's wife, Jane Shore, whose face often served for such a purpose, and so the carver may have taken his shot at both sides.

For in those days, when *Punch* was far away in the future, the church-carvers did supply the place now filled by such as Leech, or Du Maurier, or Sambourne, with their illustrations of longer vitality.

And, just here, when considering how the character of a community has grown, with that absence of break

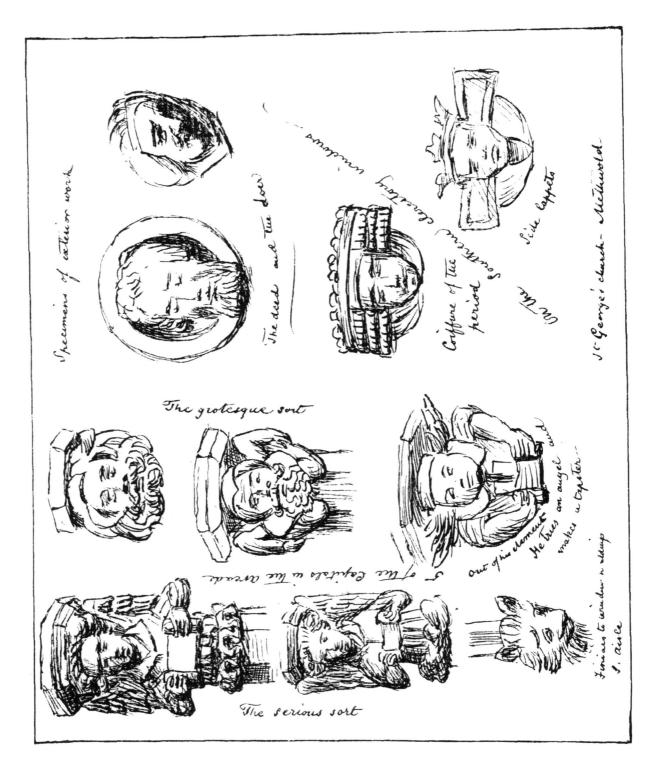

that the lamented Professor Freeman always contended for, through a lifetime of centuries; we may glance at the effect produced on the imagination, and so on the character, by architecture and its hand-maid arts, between the Saxon and Tudor periods. Architecture long played the métier of a sort of Kyrle society to the nation at large. Nurtured as it was in the bosom of the cloister, it was an advertisement and a helper of the Church; yet, we cannot study church architecture without being aware how much the love of opposition and question that dwells in human nature comes out in the suggestive incongruities of detail to which designers and carvers, both in stone and wood, lent themselves.

The influence of the builders' and carvers' guilds, that shifted, like the numerous gangs of "navvies" in later days, from town to town, or from village to village, to build or adorn churches, taking up for their assistance such as they found susceptible in the locality where they temporarily abode, was not wholly towards reverence of religion; but they were to a great extent missionaries of culture and art. As we watch the development and decadence of church architecture, we see how everything human becomes corrupt and perishes in the using. We see it grow from the simple stateliness of the Norman, through the grace of the Early English, the complexity of the Transition, the full-blown florid beauty of the Decorated, to the educated, colder, stiffer, pinching style of the Perpendicular, with the frequent secularity and unnaturalness of its ornament, both in stone and wood and in glass; and so it falls into the resigned inartistically ornate flatness of the Tudor, and, leaving a short-lived bantling in the domestic architecture of Elizabethan days, dies out for a time utterly. It is true that ecclesiastical wood carving was at its best in the Perpendicular period, but this branch of the art, as an offset of the art of figure painting, just as the work of Gibbons was of that of fruit and flower painting, had had its origin, not in architecture really, but in the recent growth of figure painting and portrait-sculpture abroad; and the utter debasement of the character of the carving in church roofs which took place in the space of a century, after it had reached its climax, shows how rapidly architecture and such art became again dissevered, the one to perish, and the other to flourish.

But, for some six centuries, architecture, and, in this country, ecclesiastical architecture mainly, had been the chief instrument for creating and spreading those ameliorating influences which the exaltation of taste produces on our complex human nature; and with its death, a fresh period of vulgarity succeeded, rapidly to efface the refining instincts of the past. Or, to put it more simply, religion had become so intimately bound up with ideas of external representation, that in reviving it on a deeper and more purely internal basis, the temporary effacement of the former sentiment became a matter of course, and perhaps of seeming necessity.

Sketch of Roof of St Georges Church, Methwold – from the Chancel

The more cultured minority, however, did not part with the worship of material beauty at once. For a time it was kept alive by transferring it to domestic uses, and it found exercise, both in Tudor domestic architecture, and, to a lesser extent, for some time longer, in furniture, and in personal dress. But it was to find its death-blow in the fact that the second Stuart sovereign was a man of taste, and that his taste should incline him towards the older and less masculine tastes in religion, whilst he should be weak in the deeper principles that are based on a reverence for abstract truth. The character and conduct of Charles I. served as an object lesson to the nation, finally to disgust it with sentimentalism; and give it a dead set towards the commonplace and the unromantic. In him the posthumous revival of past ideas served to kill them twice over in the popular sentiment, their good and their evil together; and, with his fall, taste in architecture, in dress, and manners, for a time disappeared, and the English nation began to sink towards a rough bourgoisie, for which a low-German race has no little affinity, and from which we are only now recovering.

It is almost pathetic to see in the Tudor and early Jacobean periods with what eagerness the possibilities of an inferior material, such as brick, for tasteful arrangement or moulded lineament, were still for a while seized upon, when the use of the nobler material, stone, was being abandoned, or only retained, in quoins and such like, for structural strength. It is with the blank despair of resignation that one contemplates the buildings of the later Stuart period, from which every sort of sentiment has evaporated. As a protest against something in the past, they may have served their unsightly purpose for a time in the reinvigoration of the national character; they may be the rags that helped to bring the prodigal to his senses after a good custom had corrupted itself, the husks that attracted a stomach sick of delicacies and their accompaniments; but they are an evidence of retributive disgust such as could neither be expected nor desired to be permanent.

The nation had adopted total abstinence in the matter of taste and beauty so far—alas! the starved sentiment took its revenge, with the Restoration, in the besotted worship of feminine charms. Now again, at last, under the gentler and purer tendencies of the present reign, taste has run back into the long-dry channels of innocent and elevating art; church restoration, improved taste in painting and sculpture, the more artistic and becoming dress of women, the increasing beauty of individual features, which, by a well-known sequence, originates in the more cultured tastes of the female parent, even the revived appreciation of mountain scenery, all show how the tide of taste is rising, and with it the accompanying dangers have returned so rapidly, and so influenced the sentiment of religion, that one fears sometimes lest so sturdy and matter-of-fact a race as our own should be presently moved

to oust it once more as a dangerous and enervating influence.

Yes! and in even such a community as this we may trace clearly all the influences that have made the nation. The rudeness of Keltic infancy, the proprieties of the Roman school-time, Saxon domesticity, Norman chivalry not untouched with French apishness, Tudor chill and sudden intellectualism, Stuart rashness and "finnicking" taste, Dutch practicality, Georgian coarseness, Victorian tentative recovery and frequent vacillation of sentiment, have all had their influence, and left their mark here, as in the nation at large.

Whilst speaking of ecclesiastical art, we may naturally turn to the art of engraving monumental brasses, which was at its best in the Decorated period, and in the hands of Flemish artists. We have here a fine example in the memorial laid down to Sir Adam de Clifton in 1367. In what way this family became settled in Methwold, to revive, perhaps, some of the instinct of respectful attachment that had once clung to the De Warennes, we have been unable to gather. Anyhow, the centre of the chancel was occupied with this memorial, embedded in such a noble slab of black marble, 10 ft. by 4 ft., as could hardly have been excavated far from the Meuse Valley.

The memorial originally consisted of the mailed figure of the knight, with its beautiful Gothic canopy, an encircling inscription, and coats of arms in all four corners; and is remarkable for the firm delineation of so distinctive a face, that one is drawn to believe that it must be an actual portrait, and no merely conventional representation. The illustration presents what remains of it as it now stands against the north wall of the Sanctuary. How it comes to be there, and thus, is worthy of being told; and its intermediate history is significant of much. In 1680, rather more than two centuries after its laying down, the Clifton family having already long disappeared, the effigy was torn from its matrix, and sold to a travelling brassworker at the price of old metal. But a hue and cry was immediately raised, and about two-thirds of the figure, with a considerable portion of the canopy, recovered; already broken up into small fragments, some of which had even passed the fire, and lost their alloy. These recovered fragments were, sooner or later, huddled with a general collection of oddities into a supplementary church chest; the principal chest, which is interesting for its ironwork and locks, probably of local manufacture, being reserved for documents; and they lay there till our day.

In 1680, the leading man of the parish, who, we shall find, was allowed to sign alone as representative of Methwold during the drainage war, was one Abraham Young or Younge, a member of a family that for generations held the office of parish warden. In the earliest of our registers that remains, we find one Anthony Franck—we wonder if he were connected with Robert Franck of piscatorial notoriety—vicar of the parish, with Thomas Swift and John

Younge, churchwardens. This is in 1683. On May the 22nd of that year we have the burial of Isaac Younge, churchwarden. Probably both Isaac and John were sons of the above-mentioned Abraham. The father must have pre-deceased the former by only a year or two, and the younger brother have replaced the elder by a sort of lineal succession.

Anthony Franck's signature gives the notion of an orderly, and at the same time, quick disposition; it is powerful and manly; neat, but unlaboured; compact, yet with a dash of determination. I have dreamed that the sexton who sold the brass may have counted on the collusion of the people's warden, one of the Younges anyhow, a masterful man of the people, probably of Puritan tendencies; and that Anthony Franck, backed probably by his own warden, Thomas Swift, must have caused the immediate stir that fortunately issued in its partial recovery. 1680 was a memorable year for acerbated Protestantism; it saw the indictment of the king's brother (afterwards James II.), and the excitement of the Popish plot was then rampant. The effects of the recent drainage, which we shall find had here a strangely personal connection with Charles I., the lord of Methwold Manor, had estranged the parish still more from the house of Stuart and their proclivities; the popular element must have been singularly strong, and the Younges almost local Cromwells. The inextinguishable traits of their family countenance, still to be seen on their descendants who have fallen to the tradesman and labouring classes, bear out this notion. Some families have this marked individuality, which tramples over all admixtures of other blood. At such a time, and under such patronage, a sacrilege of this kind might be expected to be condoned; and it would have required a vicar of no slight strength of character to have enforced the vehement search for and recovery of the memorial. The vicar, "Frank" in his denunciation of the sacrilege, perhaps found in his own warden one "Swift" to track out the purchaser. But Anthony Franck died in the course of a year or two, without having been able to secure the replacement of so much as he had recovered in its original position. Perhaps he found it safer to lock the fragments up for the present. So the matrix lay still denuded, and early in the present century this had come to slant so much from the horizontal, that a local mason was set to underpin it, and he, bungling his operations, ended in letting it fall bodily into the excavation he had made. This was sufficient for the parish authorities of that day; they would not go to the expense of raising it, but ordered its grave to be simply filled in and paved over; and now its exact position, confused with that of later memorials in the memory of the very aged, cannot be discovered.

For two centuries and a half the fragments of this brass were tossed about in the church chest, whilst the story of their theft and recovery still lived in parish legend. Blomefield got hold of the legend, and took a cursory glance at the fragments, I suppose;

but anyhow he very much understates the amount of them that remained. His book, however, made the public aware of their existence, and in 1860 (there is a queer concurrence in the two dates 1680 and 1860) they were produced for inspection, when the church was visited by the Archæologists of Norfolk; and loaned, on his own request, to the Secretary of the Archæological Society, in order that he might publish a drawing of them. Then at last the parish finally forgot them. When I came into my incumbency in 1873, there was but one person in the parish who could remember when or where they had last appeared, or what might have been done with them. I made application for information about them to the Secretary, who averred that he had long since returned them. Subsequently, to his own utter surprise, he discovered them stowed away in his own attic, and made them over to myself. At last, after many endeavours to have the matrix searched for and recovered, which failed for lack of funds and of certainty where to search under the new chancel floor, which was laid down some forty years since, and divested of all past memorials; at last, in 1889, with the help of my sexton, a young smith of unusual ingenuity and talent, I was enabled once more to present the memorial to the eye of the public. Each fragment, having been drilled for a couple or more of brass pins, was affixed in its proper order on a large slab of elm, round which a grove was sunk, by way of framing, a few inches in from its chamfered edge; and when the brass, so much as remained of it, was all in its place, I painted in the remainder of the effigy, and as much as was desirable for symmetry and balance of the missing parts of the canopy. Adapting the tone, or rather tones, of the colouring to the neighbouring metal, I succeeded so far in producing the impression of a complete effigy, that I have more than once had to ascertain by touch whether some portion of the painting were not actually metal. Of course the colouring is of a simple character, and the light generally not too searching.

Perhaps the trouble I have taken may plead for me, and my natural pleasure in the success of my work excuse me, for preserving here the memorial of my first sensations at seeing it completed, which I penned at the time.

> So, with that look so serious, sad, and firm,
> The ancient limner knew, upon thy face,
> Thou standest forth, for yet another term,
> Nearer God's altar than thy former place:
> Another term, a term, we trust, to last
> Till thou and we together eye to eye
> Behold Him, thoughts of Whom seem graven fast
> Upon that face in its grim panoply.
> Thou stand'st before us with wrapt solemn air,
> And a Communion with saints gone we feel,
> As, with meek hands uplift with thine in prayer,
> For foretaste of heaven's bridal feast we kneel.
> Methinks not only warrior staunch wert thou,
> But knightly soldier of a higher King,
> For deeper things are writ on lip and brow,

Than common ways of hall and camp might bring,
Kept, thus to look upon us once again.
Through thy strange history of five hundred years,
Thou gazest out, beyond earth's motley train,
Toward that which every spirit hopes or fears.
A silent monitor, dead but speaking yet,
Throughout the changeful centuries' ebb and flow,
That we may bend our thoughts, where thine are set,
For that unveiling man has yet to know.
Thy steely garb that tells of ways unknown
To us, enfolds a like humanity
To ours, we count for accident alone
Of birth the environing diversity.
Thy personal cares, thy loves, thy wonderment
O'er the unravelling of life's tangled skein,
We know them all—you did not all you meant,
Neither can we—God yet shall make all plain.

January 14*th*, 1889

CHAPTER VI.

In Tudor Times.

THE Tudor period was a time of domestic revival and advance. The idea of the home, the value of the individual human being, was strengthened. The decay of chivalry, the impoverishment and partial obliteration of the older nobility by the wars of the Roses, the transferral of dignity to new men who were anxious to win popular notice, had left the commonalty less overawed, and increased their relative importance. That revolutionary period, which was really much affected in its issues by popular opinion, was succeeded by a period of Imperialism, in which sovereignty addressed itself to the populace. The successes of the house of York were owing to popular favor: the permanence of the throne of the first Tudor, whose Keltic tendencies led him towards absolutism, really rested on the popularity of the Yorkist princess whom he had married, to whom the title of "the good Queen Bess," afterwards transferred, or supposed to have been so, to Queen Elizabeth, was originally assigned. From her, quite as much as from his Tudor ancestry,—and from her grandmother, Elizabeth Woodville, a woman of unmistakable charm,—the "Bluff King Hal" inherited qualities which, for all his terrible defects of character, preserved his popularity with the people. As by his extravagance of show and pageant, so also by that Sultanesque exercise of inclination, which led him to choose his viziers from the ranks, as well as to execute the successive tenants of his harem, he tickled the fancies of the multitude.

It was a period of revival for commerce also: wealth and importance spread to a new class, which had more access to the sovereign, as a whole, than heretofore; and the number of well-to-do people in the ranks, whose success gave hope of like advancement to others, was increased. Barriers were certainly disappearing; nothing seemed impossible to ambitious ability and industry. The lesser country magnates, who had always looked towards their poorer neighbours for sympathy, began to find their position more hopeful; and, to support themselves more on popular recognition, took to erecting moderate mansions for occasional residence within the country towns and the larger villages. Example was taken from this to erect noticeable dwellings for the secular clergy, with whom they associated themselves; and the clergy, once that, by ceasing to be celibate, they became full members of the civil community, took, here and there, more of a social position of importance. To these influences we owe the erection, during the Tudor period, of the Town House of the De Mundefords at Methwold, of the old Vicarage, and of another Tudor residence recently demolished, of all three of which we give illustrations. And there remain in Tudor brickwork and chimneys now imbedded in inferior edifices of later erection, both in the High Street and on the Fair Hill, many signs of the new growth and activity that came upon Methwold during this period. And somewhere in the last days of this period must have arisen once more a Hall, this time a house in the ordinary line of street, the New Hall, to which we shall also refer.

The English notion of "respectability," as we still understand the term, which forms so valuable, if sometimes sordid and bourgeois, an ingredient in the national character, now took root; and it has had a vast effect on the fortunes of the nation. The free publication of the Sacred Scriptures also, reminding every man of the dignity and responsibility of possessing a personal conscience and opinion; and the sudden general rise of literature which is closely connected with their study; added weight to the new tendencies, and appealed to higher human functions in the masses, than had hitherto been called upon.

Legend began to give way to information, which was at least taken for veracious; religion had to bear the brunt of discussion; philosophy was to be formulated by Sir Francis Bacon; poets were to produce philosophical, historical, and political lessons in reflection or forecast, instead of merely painting present phenomena with Chaucer or Piers Plowman. So long as the fresh study of the Scriptures gave a new motive to thought, England walked in a new dream of the dignity of humanity, which showed itself even in the stateliness and decorum of private life. The fantasies of chivalry were replaced by patriarchal and apostolic notions, which were stiff, and sometimes a little grotesque.

The pomposity of the period affected its diction, and is preserved in our Bibles; it was a symptom and a preservative; and was, and is, more suited to Englishmen than the French elegance, with its frivolity, introduced by the Restoration; better for us, too, perhaps, than the slanginess, and worse, reflected on us, in these days, by our Indian and Colonial connection. Like the Roman, the Englishman requires the support of "dignitas," being inclined to fall into gaucherie; he makes a sorry gallant and a blundering buffoon, but he has the severer virtues, which, if they are apt to become perverted through a tendency to prejudice, can be softened by Charity and beautified by real culture. He is a weighty being, and possesses more affinity with the nobler domestic animals, than with those feline or other classes of the feræ naturæ, to whom elegance is natural, rather than dignity.

It was quite in character with Methwold taste, too, that the religious head of the community should be becomingly housed. Methwold has always retained a sensible care for appearances; after many years of desolating depression, though her yeomen are gone from their lands, and her farm-houses are occupied by stewards; though her village girls troop up to the towns, and the youths follow after them; though a girl in her teens does, with the assistance of the mistress, the work of a pair of adult domestics; still dilapidated buildings or broken walls are not to be endured; still homes are kept orderly by greatly increased effort; still every Fair Day sees the place lightened up and smiling under a new coat of the prevalent ochre of a warm orange tint; and Methwold never ceases to hold on by the motto:—*Durate et rebus vosmet servate secundis.* The bricklayer and the carpenter are always over-full of work still, though the gardener finds it hard to live; and reductions are made in the way of pleasures, rather than of respectability.

It was during the Tudor period, as is evident by the tone of the mouldings, and by its character as a whole, that the present porch was somewhat badly joined on to the wall of the south aisle of the church.

I am inclined, from observation in many places, to conjecture, that, where no Guild Hall existed, these porches, so frequently added in Tudor times, were built for Guild meetings, rather than for vestries, to which they were given up later. Sometimes, where one porch already existed, we find a second added at this date to the other aisle,—it is so at Mildenhall—

as if for a new and definite purpose. The Guilds of those days were the ancestors of our trade companies, and benefit clubs, and even of our trades unions, and then always stood in connection with the church. The Church had never quite lost its popular instincts, and has had more to do, at all times, with the nurturing of popular institutions than is generally allowed. Magna Charta would never have been signed, had not Stephen Langton given countenance and direction to the constitutional idea.

The abbey of Bury welcomed in John's reign the army of the Dauphin, lying hard by on Haberdon, as much out of sympathy with the people, as out of collusion with the Pope. The popular movements in the reign of Richard II. could not have advanced so far but for the countenance of many of the secular clergy. When once, to gain help in the prosecution of heresy, the Church cast in its lot with the usurping and unpopular house of Lancaster; which, just for the sake of Church support, adopted the persecuting rôle, so strange in the descendants* of John of Gaunt; the royal house and the Church establishment were alike pre-doomed for the day, when, out of the failures of Church and Crown, should arise the authority of the national conscience. Now that the people have learned to stand alone, popular institutions can surely

---

* Close observation of the procedure of the House of Lancaster, from the days of Edward II., shows them always to have occupied the same position towards the reigning branch as the Orléans family have done in France.

afford to look back to their religious origin; and it were well if they were still always moderated by the principles of religion. It is as unjust to forget that there were brotherhoods before the Reformation connected with the Church, as that there were village schools before the Education Act. Nor must we be too prejudiced to own that many good things fell for awhile into abeyance with the Reformation, having lost the guiding hand, and the often munificence, of the Church. Many institutions, social, charitable, and educational, suffered severely. Every revolution is something of a return to darkness, though it be the eve of a new and better day. When we mark the traces of Guild chapels in the aisles here, and conjecture the possible first uses of the porch, we thank God for our forefathers, remembering that institutions framed on a basis of brotherly union and mutual support are not new things under the sun. The Reformation had its bad things, some of which we may not yet have thoroughly found out; even the free publication of the Scriptures was not at first altogether beneficial. The religious inconsistencies of Puritanism arose, in the absence of Biblical science, from a misapplication of Old Testament example. If the clergy of the older Church had been interested and dishonest in their doling out of the truth of the Bible, the people's folly in their misunderstanding of it was, for long, hardly less mischievous.

The reversion to Church tyranny under Laud was not without its intelligible and even good motive;

but it failed, as all endeavours will fail, to put back the clock of time. Again, as Pharisaism arose out of the recent compilation and publication of the Hebrew Canon, so Puritanism arose out of the free dissemination of the "whole Word of God"; and they are not without their sinister points of comparison. And, as in later Jewish days the choice lay between the Pharisaism of the masses, and the Saduceeism of the Temple; so, when Puritanism had exhausted the national patience, there was only too much of the Saducee about the Churchman of the Restoration. Human progress, even religious progress, is made by alternate steps and stoppages. Now this instinct, and now that, falls into abeyance; only Charity, reverencing, and not scorning the past; welcoming, and not distrusting the future; can form a bond of perfectness, uniting all virtues.

It is the safeguard of the English nation that the older instinct never quite perishes, and is often reverted to; and about this time an old instinct, that of kindly affection towards indwellers of the higher class, had opportunities of revival in Methwold. Evil always arises from the opposition of classes; good, from their admixture and contact. Out of social admixture and mutual human sympathy arises the best kind of socialism; and there is really more of socialism about our institutions than can be found anywhere else, after all. Therefore it was good for Methwold that the De Mundefords, and others like them, should have about this time built houses, and taken up their abode, in the town.

But, in speaking of the domestic residences of the period that remain, I will speak first of the old Vicarage, as that which is most worthy of description.

The sketch I give of it is greatly taken from a very ingenious model of what it would be if fully restored, executed in oak, under my advice, by the sexton who worked with me on the Clifton brass. The projecting windows of the upper storey to the west do not exist; but the places of their insertion are evident from within. The carved posts of the ground floor remain, but we had to pick out the plaster and colouring with which they are defaced, to discover their beautiful workmanship and ornament. The brickwork of the gable remains perfect, and shewed as in the sketch when I drew it a few years since—now, alas! the tenant of one of the two cottages into which it is divided has been allowed to smother it with ivy. Oh! if some nightly visitant would but sever the stems of that accursed plant. Why should a community have no power against private vandalism? Oh! if my predecessor, instead of erecting my vicarage house out of contact with the village, at one end of this enormous parish of nearly 14,000 acres, had but accepted, as he might have done at a very low price, the New Hall adjoining, and secured the old Vicarage for parish rooms, for clubs, for mothers' meetings, for G. F. S., and other such uses, restoring the two long apartments of which it consists to their old dimensions,

by only pulling out the rough partitions knocked up midway. Oh! if some charitable millionaire even now would buy it, and its price would be very small, and present it to the parish. As it is, the New Hall was bought directly after by a worthy citizen, who congratulates himself on the insertion of brilliant white sashes in place of the mullioned windows he found there; and the same has been done in the two lower stories of the vicarage gable.

The vicarage, probably a thatched building originally, had then three floors; a tiled roof now has been put on, which has virtually eliminated the top floor. The two lower floors consisted each of but one large apartment. The sketch opposite gives an idea of the lower one, and of the staircase by which, judging by indications, the upper must have been reached. The mantelpiece shown there is drawn from that which still, in the early days of my incumbency, adorned the upper chamber. That in this had long been cleared away, and its place re-modelled to cottage uses. The roof-beams of the apartment are richly moulded; whilst carving that takes the form of a crumpled riband, volute round a staff, and bound at intervals, lies in the deep central groove of its lower face. The beams of the upper floor are more simply moulded. The chimney of the lower room is external in the centre of the gable, and is of very ornate brickwork, divided into stages of different pattern, as will be seen by the drawing. The gables are the only brick part of the structure, its back and front being framed in timber, with chalk and plaster filling. On either side of the chimney stack in both chambers are windows approached by deep recesses with arched ceilings; those in the upper room are supplied with seats recessed into the walls. There seems to have been but one other window in the lower chamber, opposite the staircase, the site of which is now enclosed within a pantry partitioned off from the keeping-room of the further cottage, but it must have appeared originally as in the second drawing.

The attic storey, now no longer existing, may have contained several chambers. If this residence, which might even have been erected in the reign of Henry VII., was thus originally intended for a celibate vicar, we need not, any the more, wonder at an arrangement which would have compelled his housekeeper to pass through the one large chamber on her way to her own apartment. For many considerable country mansions of the next reign, or even that of Elizabeth, are so built that the one broad staircase ends in, and again rises from, the principal sleeping apartment. Probably a screen round the bed obviated all actual indelicacy in this arrangement, which was intended to keep the household, once retired to the upper floor, under ward: much as the Irish peasant, having arranged his family, girls inmost, chance strangers outside, on the floor of his cabin, for the night, takes up his post of observation.

I give opposite a drawing of a portion of a late

Party Elizabethan bed's head rescued from burning by the Vicar

Tudor bedstead, the head-piece, which I found a labourer just about to break up for firewood, that once doubtless had its place in one or other of the houses of that period. The tenant of the vicarage house who aggravates me with his ivy, had already cleared away the beautiful moulded brick side-posts of the chamber fireplace, and heaped them with his other rubble, when I purchased of him the beautiful mantel also condemned to the fire. The oak cradle which I shall give in, and which belongs, properly speaking, to the Stuart period, for it is dated, as will be perceived, 1660, came into my hands in more tragic fashion. With regard to all such objects, I will delay my tale for a moment to say, that it would be well if the Society for the Preservation of Ancient Monuments kept a fund in hand for the recouping of poor vicars and such like, who wrest them from destruction, and who would in that case pass them over to some museum established for the purpose. As to this cradle, then, it had drifted about amongst the cottagers, and formed a feature at their petty sales for centuries, before I at last came upon it in the outhouse of a minute two-storied cottage, whither it had been hastily carried, with one pannel already split and burning. For the occupants of this tiny cottage, a very aged couple, addicted to a habit that is now happily becoming less common in the Fen country, of soothing the troubles of a blank senility with opium, having left a candle alight too near to their bed curtains, had unconsciously laid themselves down for the last time alive. The curtain nearest the light had heated till it took fire, after the smouldering fashion of tinder, their unnatural slumber held them unaware of it; and when in the morning the attention of neighbours was drawn to the smoke issuing from every crack and cranny of their dwelling-box, and the door forced in, and way made, at risk of suffocation, into the chamber, the old lady was found already dead of suffocation, and the partner of her joys and sorrows an hour later shared her fate. A woman who had sat with the old lady, who had been "keeping her bed" on the previous day, had brought her infant with her and her cradle, and when she left at night time, removed the infant but not the cradle, which she was glad to receive the means of replacing by a more modern and removable contrivance.

The house of the De Mundefords, which stands on the east side of the Fair Hill, blocked from view by one of the houses that have grown up, by gradual encroachment, out of the booths of the Fair, as in some cases may be proved, here, and in many other localities, from the title deeds, shews how the notion of a more complete domestic arrangement was at this period evolving itself. The home within was being improved, whilst at the same time its exterior architecture was rapidly deteriorating; thus we have a sign of national change tending towards utilitarianism and real convenience, and accompanied, alas! by a withdrawal of attention from appearances, that was to produce evil consequences presently; for the pre-

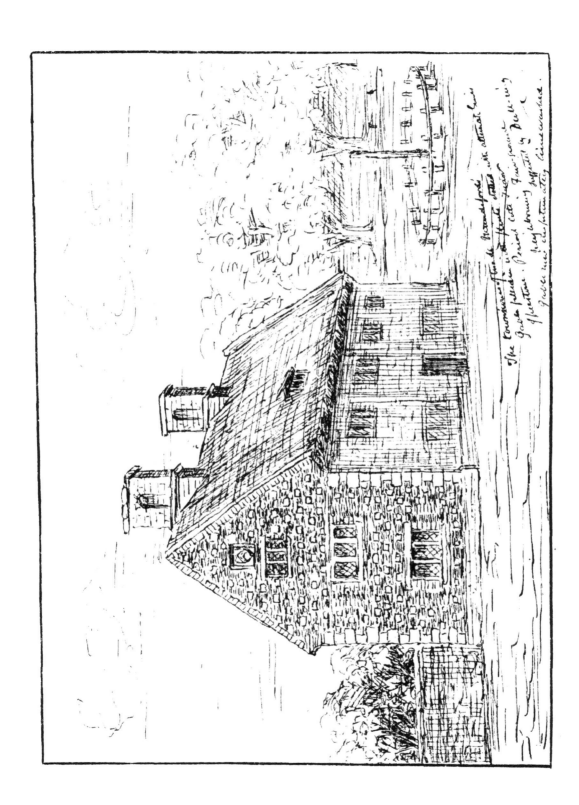

serving of "things with a fair appearance (*a. v.* honest) in the sight of all men" has a deep moral effect, as the inspired Apostle perceived when he urged it on his converts. How sad it is that humanity can rarely grasp a new truth without dropping some old one.

These De Mundefords took their name from the neighbouring village of Mundford, which also is interesting as containing a fine specimen of the original mound on which the British "set" was planted, that enclosed a quadrangular area, intersected by a small stream. The mansion house of the place, higher up, was surrounded by a double stockade. The present village street lies at one end of the quadrangle. The De Mundefords had property also at Feltwell, and their memorials are in the church of that parish, to which they left considerable charities; but they had this town house in our midst. A study of the beautiful gable to the south, chequered with flint-work and with stone, probably from remains of the residence of the De Warennes, leads one to the conclusion that it is of the date of Henry VIII. Above the attic window in this gable we find their coat of arms set within a frame of moulded brick-work, similar in character to that which surrounds the arms of Charles Brandon, on the house where he resided with Mary Tudor, at West Stow in Suffolk.

One steps down quite a couple of feet, by stone steps within the low entrance, to the ground floor of the De Mundeford house. This error in house construction * died hard—it is instanced in many much more considerable residences of the period. The lowest storey is thus rendered extremely low in its external aspect. The door opened on the principal apartment, the living hall, in fact; but the other two apartments into which the space is divided, and between which the staircase was carried up, and not out of the hall, are entered by a narrow passage running from the furthermost end of the hall, beside the rear wall of the house. Probably the larger apartment at the south end was the servants' room and kitchen, and the smaller apartment was for the ladies, who, in Queen Anne's time, would have been provided with a large day-room on the next floor. So again, the staircase lands, not into the principal chamber, which is over part of the hall at the north end, but on a narrow passage against the front wall. But the heads of the household had to pass through a chamber occupying the whole width of the house, above the ladies' day-room, to reach their own. A third chamber occupies the space over the kitchen, and there are sleeping-rooms for the servants above in the thatched roof, the one lighted by a dormer which retains much of its original moulded wood-work; the other by the window in the gable. It is a simple abode, and ill finished within; the hearth-stones of the chambers are set in a neatly-carved oak

---

* Here, singularly enough, it characterizes also the church.

border, but otherwise all is very rough; the walls are such as only the hangings could render sightly, and everything is of the plainest, but still the idea of privacy is growing. The windows, now roughly filled up and replaced by larger ones cut in new positions, were long and low; all but one, nearly against the north gable, disclosed with its original woodwork by the falling off of mortar, that must have lighted a closet partitioned off a corner of the principal chamber, thus forming a primitive dressing-room for the mistress or master of the house. Probably the screen that separated it was of wood-work only. This window of a single pane, only recently disclosed, is not indicated in the drawing. The fact of a country dignitary erecting a town house in so small a place as Methwold is a sign of the times. The gentry were drawing nearer to the commonalty. Perhaps the house with a Tudor gable, recently demolished near the George Inn, and another of which the remnants of the chimneys and some of the ornamental brick front now embedded in cottages indicate the existence, originated in a similar tendency. The chimneys that arise out of the roofs of the line of cottages opposite the south front of the church are also Tudor. Following these indications, we perceive that at this date the village had encircled the new church and the Fair Hill, deserting greatly the hollow; but beyond this, where a great part of the village now lies, to the eastward, there is no trace of early residence. In fact we have here a "west end" to Methwold, being, in fact, the east end, and the idea of a quartier for the upper class inhabitants in immediate contact with the villagers is established. What the presence of the residence of some noble did for the serfs and dependents of an earlier date, such contiguity now did, without the disadvantage of so mighty a contrast in condition. In fact approximation had rendered what contrast there remained elevating and stimulating, instead of depressing, in its effect.

Of course the gentry would reside here principally at Fair time, for pleasure as well as for business. No doubt some of the amusements which then pleased all classes together, were coarse, and not worthy of enlightened patronage. To civilize amusements is the last touch of social progress; yet we wish that the gentry had kept touch with the villagers in their sports, and so retained the power to modify their character. Puritanism, which, when it abolished the religion of the cloister, carried its spirit into private life, has too much left vulgar amusement to the vulgar— and to the devil. The task of undoing the effect of this is the hardest task that falls to the clergy in the country, and has only lately been taken up. I can remember when we considered ourselves at liberty to read Dickens and Thackeray at home, but bound to assure our poorer neighbours that they needed no literature but the Holy Scriptures. In fact we ignored altogether their entertainment, so that all amusement of their dull lives fell under the ban of the parson, and was entered on in the mistaken spirit of the thought that God has nothing to do with human mirth and enjoyment.

The modern Fair is a pitiful and paltry thing, less lively, but hardly less demoralizing than in the days of bull-baiting and such like. And the amusements of our town poor, their music halls and such like, are mostly demoralizing. Had the gentry still shared, through the last three centuries, in the merry-makings of the multitude, instead of leaving them to themselves, they might by this time have raised their character; and the nature of their amusements is the truest test of the moral standard of a community. It has been a mistake to associate ourselves with our poorer neighbours only in religious matters; and, in consequence, they naturally imagine that, when we return to an interest in their pleasures, we are lowering our religious standard; and it is hard to infect them with the principles we endeavour to bring into them with us. But if we are to improve the root and occasion of a thousand evils, we must get an influence over, by taking a part, wherever possible, in, their amusements.

It remains to take notice of the house known as the New Hall. This, which is a considerable house, on the opposite side of the High Street from the Old Hall Close, below the old vicarage, is probably of late Elizabethan date. Externally, since its front has been marred by the introduction of sash windows, it possesses little interest save in the eastern gable, which is built in diamonds of red brick filled in with flint; the stone of the castle, which was probably finally used up in the adornment of the De Mundford gable, being no longer available. For whom it was built seems impossible to ascertain.* Our registers give us no help, as they commence only in 1683.

But the interior arrangements are worth studying as showing the growth of the domestic idea. The apartment, now partly portioned off for an office, which with its neighbours was panelled, upon which the door opens, was probably the principal living chamber, and the main staircase opens directly out of it, but it has a large apartment on either side of it: these between them fill up the ground space. In the one the whole family would probably have been found associated, except at meal-times; the other was

---

* This house was once in the occupation of Rear-Admiral Manby, the inventor of the rocket-apparatus for saving life on the sea-coast; whose manservant, Nayler, I remember still in possession of every faculty but that of hearing, at the age of 114 years, when I entered upon the charge of Ten-Mile-Bank in Hilgay, in 1864.

Nayler died about three years after, aged 117. The longevity of such of the Fen population as survived the thrush in infancy, and the ague in youth, is well known. I found that shortly before this date, at South Hilgay (now St. Johns', Little Ouse), the death of a patriarch of 106 had killed his life-partner, who "had the better of him," that is, was the senior of him by one year, so quickly, that the one burial did for both.

Racing in my light boat as far as Denver sluice one day, I saw a well-known character, who was trundling above me on the high bank the wheelbarrow in which he was in the habit of conveying bricks and mortar five miles, from Downham, when any small repairs were needed to his cottages on "The Bank"; and afterwards walking beside him along the St. John's-Ea at my best pace into town, I learned that he was the senior of a woman of 87, whom I had that day buried; and that his father, having married his third wife at 103, outlived her, and died at 112. But the village churchyards of the district present many like instances.

Bedroom fireplaces of Tudor period at Methwold
1. Stone mantel carved with hearts and 7 chevrons in old farmhouse (added to and remodelled) in Globe Street
2, 3 - Hearth-curbs, oaken in the De Mundeford house

probably the kitchen. The arrangements of the first floor show something like modern ideas of household convenience, and the attic floor is lofty and habitable.

There is yet another house standing on the north side of the street that bordered the back of the Hall Close, which, to a casual observer, would betoken little enough of interest. A respectable farm-house of moderate height, roofed with slate, and fitted throughout with sash windows, with a slip of grass and flower-beds in front guarded by an iron railing. No one would credit it with what quality of eld it hides within, or suppose that it could have anything to attract the antiquarian. Yet, even without, it will reward a searching examination, for, on looking closer to the smiling, coloured face, one detects every here and there that older openings have been filled in from time to time, and comes, as in a palimpsest, upon the traces of its original features. Within, if one ascends the modern staircase, and takes the passage to its western end, one finds oneself in the remains of a large Tudor chamber, of which a part has been cut off for smaller apartments, still floored with the original oak, and still containing the very interesting mantelpiece figured opposite. And this house was still, till quite recently, regarded as the superior in dignity of all the houses of the place; in some sort its manor-house; so that whosoever happened to be its tenant, was, by virtue of his residence, charged with the solemn guardianship of the parish maps and such like. It is possible that this may have been originally the seat of the Cliftons, to one of whom the brass of 1367, figured in connection with the church, was laid down. I have not had an opportunity of tracing the Clifton arms, and therefore cannot say if their insignia are to be compared with the ornamentation of the mantel, which is so singular that it can hardly be void of some significance. This will be seen, from the illustration, to consist of seven chevrons and a heart,—repeated on the chamfered edge of either jamb and twice over on that of the crosspiece above, so that there the two hearts came into near conjunction—a happy symbol of union for the chamber of a married pair—suggesting, in the one case, the two individualities, each with a well-guarded heart to give the rule to their behaviour through all seven days of the week; in the other, those hearts united over the domestic hearth, with each day's troubles, guarded and regarded, when brought there, only as true affection should dictate.

Cradle in wainscoat marked P.F. 1666
probably brought into the Parish by
Anthony Frauck, Vicar
1670 to 1688
in the possession of the present Vicar

CHAPTER VII.

In Stuart Times.

IN our last chapter we have adverted somewhat to the bad side of Puritanism. The revulsion from Puritanism, with many, is in these days intemperate already, so that it needs not to be strengthened; but it is foolish to be blind to the defects of any order of ideas. The Stuart era saw the growth of Puritanism, which had perhaps had its first origin with the Lollards; and also the use of a new dissoluteness in England. Strange to say, both owed something to religious discussion.

Elizabeth had finally established, in name at least, a National Church in close dependence on the State. Loyalty to herself as a Protestant champion, and patriotism against Spain, helped to save the new institution from criticism. But the Church, being no longer a part of the general ecclesiastical body of Western Europe, felt the chill of isolation. Its first leanings were towards foreign Protestantism, and its then most powerful representative, Calvin. The succession of James prepared it for still further tendencies in the same direction, but James himself presently checked the movement.

From the nature of her establishment, a too great aquiescence in the proclivity of the sovereign might have been prognosticated. Her danger lay in the timidity with which she ran alone, and every swerve she made brought danger to the nation. Motives of kingcraft, in which he fancied himself an adept, speedily drew James to the support of the Catholic party in convocation; and the disappointment, and presently the disaffection of a large body of earnest Protestants was the result.

This exterior influence ruined the chance of interior harmony. When the Independents had disgusted the nation by their rudeness and tyranny over the national conscience, and the Presbyterians had figured as enemies of both sides in the course of the civil war, the re-establishment of the Anglican Church was hailed as a relief, and new safeguards for her supremacy accepted. Alas! it was expected of her that she should lighten the weight of religion on the conscience, and the idea of the Church became mixed up with the idea of loyalty to monarchical government; whilst the example of the king as her head and patron tended to lower the tone of her religion, and further to alienate those of Puritan leanings. But, as Puritanism had arisen from a desire to safeguard the conscience against laxity or supposed error; so dissoluteness probably began, unconsciously, out of the sense that an enforced general sanctity savoured of hypocrisy, if it did not promote it. The Church of the nation should, from the first, have set herself solemnly to bear the weight of her own responsibility, and she might have become truly representative and preservative of the national conscience, and a real and trusted authority to replace that of Rome; instead of remaining as she has done, a congeries of parties mutually dissident. Neither should she in this case have countenanced the imprudences of Charles I., nor been dragged down by the laxities of the later Stuart and the Georgian eras. It is doubtful whether she ever did half as much for the support of religion for a long time after the Restoration, as the Church of Rome had done through the long days of Norman and Plantagenet. Consequently the fear of hypocrisy rapidly ran on to a pretty general laxity of morals, accompanied or not by religious formalism.

The character of the second Charles extended its malign infection even to Methwold, backed, as we shall see, by his personal presence, when he paid a flying visit to the place; induced, if legend be true, by no such respectable reasons as a desire to make acquaintance with his personal property.

But already, from the times of James I., there had been business on hand in connection with the Royal Manor, which affected the loyalty and other sentiments of the community.

We must now turn our eyes to the Fen portion of the parish, of which we have reserved the consideration until now. Some two-thirds of the parish is actually fen, even if we exclude that arm of the fen which extended once to Cranwich, under the name of the Poteye's ford or Pottisford. It was during the Stuart era that the most determined efforts were made and sustained to modify the condition of the lowland, or "Flat" as it seems to have been then called, perhaps because the Dutch engineers of the period so styled it. Now, again, the term has disappeared, and we have reverted to the distinction of Field and Fen; but the large number of families in the parish bearing the surname of Flatt shows how prevalent it must once have been, whilst the surname of "Fen" or "Fenn," so common in West Suffolk, does not exist amongst us.

The fen, then, or flat of Methwold, forms the northern half of the basin lying between the streams of the Wissey to the north and the Little Ouse to the south and west, of which the western portion afterwards became part of the main stream of the Great Ouse. Both Ouse and Wissey are representatives of that Keltic word for water, which the Saxons, or tribal varieties of Britons, have handed down to us as Ouse and Usk; as Exe, and Oxe, and Axe; as Wis and Wissey—perhaps the latter is a diminutive—but which the Romans write either as Isa, or Usa, or Isis. This basin had about its centre a natural drain of its own, a small stream, issuing from two sources, the

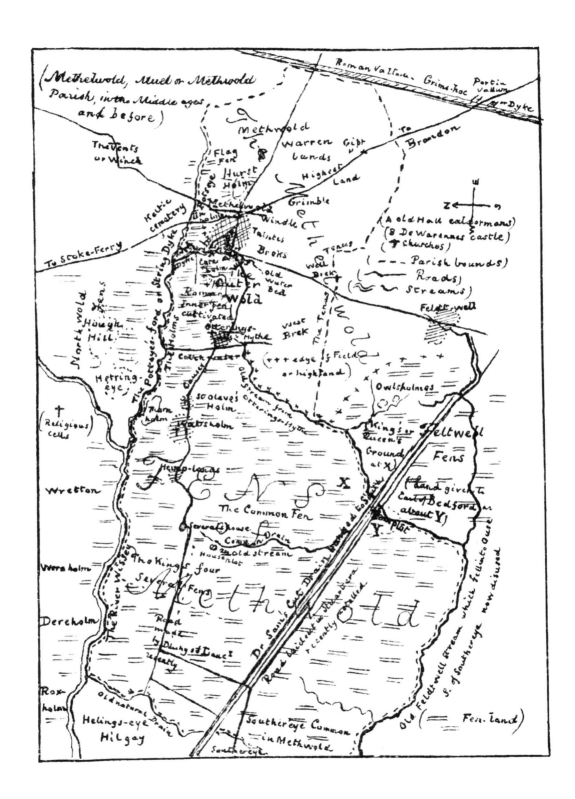

one the Feldt-well, the other by the chalk rise south of Ottering-hythe, but running as a single stream from Powplot or Poplot, now corrupted into Poppylot. This stream, traced from its source at Ottering-hythe,* formed, and its original course still forms, the southern boundary of Methwold. Another small stream that rose out of Heling's-eye and fell into this, where it sidled round the S.E. corner of Southereye, formed most of the western boundary of the parish. But

---

* Since the earlier chapters of this work were put in print, Mr. J. J. Coulton, in his interesting *Notes on the Names on the Wissey*, has published certain views regarding this hamlet that require notice. First, as to the variety of the name, which makes it, now an eye (island), now a hythe, landing-place. This seems to be explained by the position which the church leads us to allot to the first settlement. It lay to the north and north-east of the present hamlet, along both sides of what must have been once a shallow stream like that of Buntings, separating an island (the Hangings) from the mainland. Next, as to the supposed evacuation of the settlement on behalf of Brummel Priory. The Priory lands, now the Abbey Farm, do not cover the Church Piece, or the Hangings; the De Warennes established their right to the church patronage, and there is no evidence of their having ever ceased to be a population clear of the Priory. Lastly, as to the derivation of the name. I gave to Oder and Otter the meaning of "black," but cannot now verify my authority. If we take it to mean water, how is it that, whilst Anglo-Saxon water has become High-German wasser—otter, the name of the animal, is still so written in German? The Roman writing of the name of the river Oder was Viadus, pronounced Waidus nearly (*c.f.* via, way). This gives the sound found in German "Waid," British "Woad," a dark blue color; and, if Otter signify slate-blue or black, it would well designate the appearance of the animal still so called in water. Colors were early used as marks of septs or tribes, and there would be little distinction in calling a sept "the Waterings." The family now bearing that name, to whom Mr. Coulton refers, likely took it, at much later date, from their homestead, or their employment. If the suggested connection between hodder and water can be established, it would, however, be interesting, from its resemblance to such Greek forms as hudor (water), and idros (sweat), which are traced to the Sanscrit "svid." Perhaps the question might be decided by examination into such names as Otterburn (? Blackburn), and Otterington in Yorkshire and Durham.

Dr. Sams with his 20-ft. drain tapped both sources, the one near the west end of Feltwell, the other where it fell in at Poplot, and left the whole loop of the stream thence to Southereye to starve; and, cutting through the Stourbridge clay between Helingseye and the islet of Modingseye (Modney), carried the waters by a straight line into the Ouse bed well to the north of Southereye. I say the Ouse bed, for, as I have noted, it is so now. We have shown that Methwold Fen was drained in Roman times; certainly the Pottisford, which was within their catchwater; probably, also, the outer fen, by the clearing of the mouth of its natural drain. The Lesser Ouse, then, and long after, ran, with a fair fall, in a bed abundantly deep and capacious for its waters; the Wissey, on the contrary, was impeded by a bar at Ford-holme, and must long have presented a succession of lakes; and we would think the Romans must have erected a bank along our northern border. Anyhow the condition of our fen must again have greatly deteriorated, otherwise the Otterings could not have called their settlement a hythe or landing-place; or the sanctuaries, early connected with the hythe by a causey (chausée), have been made on St. Olave's and St. Catherine's holmes. But I have often thought there must have been another and a natural cause for the going back of the fens from the fourth century, viz., a sinking of the general surface. It is plain, from the remains of vast forests, mainly of oak and yew, strewn in one direction as by a sudden inpour, a few feet below the surface of the moor, that such sinkings had occurred before; and that in neolithic times,—as is proved by the implements found with them,—may not a last movement of a slighter character have occurred, the last throw of the convulsion (if we except the last earthquake on the Essex shore, and perhaps the recent subsidence at Sandwich), similar to that which made England an island. Probably the earlier movements were very sudden and violent, as the massing together of the bones of the woolly elephants, who had fled to their refuge on the Galloper and Shipwash sands, seems to prove.

After that the land must again have slowly risen; for in 1608 we hear of a work being undertaken to ascertain the depth of the sill of a very ancient sluice at the mouth of the run from Modney, into which Dr. Sams subsequently led the Feltwell stream, which proved that the Little Ouse bed had risen 9 ft. since its laying down, probably through the lifting of its bed seaward; and we shall presently see that, for centuries before the Stuart era, Methwold fen had been good for winter as well as for summer pasture. But, already, another natural cause had imperilled its value, the effects of which were now to be enhanced by a mistaken system of drainage.

In the thirteenth century, the Great Ouse, which originally bounded the County of Norfolk, and emptied by Wisbech, found its way, through recent drains, into the Little Ouse bed near Littleport; and thenceforward ran out at Lynn, widening and at the same time filling up the bed of the Little Ouse.

Commissions were issued in 1292 (Edward I.) and 1392 (Richard II.) to attempt the returning of the Ouse to its former bed, and to embank the lower course of Little Ouse, but they came to nothing. In 1391 we learn that the invaded stream ran a mile wide above Lynn, and was proportionately shallow, whilst incursions from the sea had ruined a vast amount of pasture. No serious enterprise was taken in hand for two centuries after this, till, in 1605, Lord Popham took in hand the work of cutting a new bed for the Ouse from Erith in Huntingdonshire to Denver, so as to relieve the pressure on the level above Denver, in which Methwold Fen is included. We find a Sir Oliver Cromwell,* who was an uncle of the future Protector, on Popham's Commission. His name appears also after a petition from Marshland in 1618, in which the damage done by an inundation five years before is estimated at £30,000. On a second commission

---

* Sir Oliver Cromwell of Hinchinbroke, uncle and godfather of the Protector, whose pet ape is recorded to have once risked the life of the future ruler by carrying him off to the house-top, was the eldest son and successor of Sir Henry Cromwell, who is reputed to have received his soubriquet of the Golden Knight on account of his liberality to the poor; but probably some truer explanation might be discovered. Sir Oliver was several times an entertainer of royalty, and was held in great reverence by James I.

Elizabeth Steward of Ely, mother of the Protector, was descended from the third son of Alexander, Lord High Steward of Scotland; as James I. was from the eldest son of the same, on his mother's side, and from the second son through his father, Darnley.

Popham's system was regarded as a failure, and his new river closed by order of Government in 1609.

In the petition from Marshland above mentioned, complaint is made of the evil result of the heightening of hardes, that is made fords, across the Ouse bed, which held back the silt. In 1608 a similar complaint had been made of the filling up of the Wissey bed, through the raising of the harde connecting Ford-holme and Helingseye. The complaint comes, as might have been expected, from Methwold. The Commission of 1618 entrusted the drainage of these fens to Sir William Ayloff and Anthony Thomas, Esq. (we are already within the Stuart era), and at first authorized those gentlemen to recoup themselves for their work by taking possession of a set portion of the improved lands, varying in localities from a tenth to even a third; in Methwold it amounted to a fourth. But in 1620, Ayloff and Thomas were summoned to a Council held before the King in Whitehall, and James stated that there was nothing in his prerogative to enable him to sanction such a grant; and that they must be satisfied with the payment of the moiety of the profit accruing to the lands on the estimation of the owners. On this the drainage was abandoned, and the fen men rejoiced in a triumphant lampoon that still remains as a literary curiosity. Nor does it appear that Methwold can have suffered much thus far, since we learn that in 1604 the king possessed here several fens (the Methwold severals) leased to Sir Edward Mundeford, who gysted (Fr. *gîter:* cattle so placed out are said to be "agist," Fr. *à gîte*) 800 beasts upon them. And in 1640, the petition which the dominant Abraham Younge penned, or signed, single-handed, for Methwold, against "the late drainage," speaks of 1700 sheep and "3 or 400" (*sic*) beeves as having been fed on the Common Fen between the Severals and Otteringhythe, both in summer and winter (another small, natural stream which fell into the Feltwell river, now known as the Common Drain, divided these fens) until the unfortunate erection of the dam at Denver by Sir Cornelius Vermuyden had been favoured and permitted by Charles I. This erection was the artificial cause of the subsequent deterioration of our Fen, to which I referred; and it was altogether a sin against right principles of drainage. Immense opposition had been offered to it at the time. Some declared that the damming of a natural stream amounted to a breaking of Magna Charta; but, under pressure from the king in person, the proposal was carried by a single vote. Many subsequent petitions were offered for its removal. But, unfortunately, the plea rested on was that damage was said to be done to Lynn Haven; and this could not be maintained, for Vermuyden had re-opened, and subsequently doubled, Popham's Cut from Erith, and the result had been a better scour through the Lynn outlet. But sufficient water still found its way round by Littleport, to be held up by the dam at Denver, and to damage the fens on the right bank of what was the original stream of the Little Ouse, whose bed has ever since been rising from the accumulation of silt.* Abraham Younge was in the right; and Methwold was with him, and against the king and his favourite, Vermuyden. The king had damaged, not only his own Severals, but their Common fen also. With the rise of the Protector, the nephew and namesake of their old Commissioner, they hoped and tried for a reversal of Vermuyden's system. Cromwell was petitioned in 1614, and gave fair words, but never found the time for going into the matter. It is curious to note that Cromwell's mother was a Stewart, and that some of her family are buried on this fen border at Lakenhythe (Lakenheath). By this matter of the drainage, Charles I. had presented Methwold with an excellent delineation of himself, which was not overlooked. A scheming idealist, and a man of fair intentions, but prejudiced and unfortunate in his predilections; first headlong in resolve, and then tenacious to unscrupulousness, he had acted like himself. To Methwold Vermuyden was as Strafford, just impeached.

---

* This fen, with those of Hilgay, Hockwold, and Southerey, again became a lagoon, on the occasion of what is still known as the "Great Drown," which was occasioned by a break of the north bank of the Little Ouse stream, during a period of very unusual rainfall, on the night of November 15th, 1852. The Drown lasted far into 1853. One curious result was the driving of vast broods of vipers to take refuge in every hedge, and on every gate-post that rose above the water level.

An old man has told me how once, intending to bind his punt to some bushes near an old house-place by the common-drain, he was fairly scared off by "them nasty adders, which was thicker in the hedge than birds in the spring."

Unfortunately, like some of the animals in the ark, that wouldn't have been missed, sufficient adders survived the exposure to renew the race.

In damming our waters, had he not set aside the great Charter? and in assigning a portion of our lands to the adventurers, had he not, in the expressed opinion of his own father, stretched the royal prerogative? For 400 solid acres of our fen, by Powplot, had been handed over to the Earl of Bedford to make up the 95,000 acres assigned to him by the king; and were not 12,000 acres of these to go as a bribe to the king himself? Perhaps the plot further up the fen, but not far away, known as the King's (or Queen's) Grounds, may have been included in these last. Anyhow, had not Charles here also been guilty not merely of a wrong, but still worse, of a blunder; and hurt himself, and his tenants and copyholders also?

Charles II. gave us his harmful countenance, and displayed towards us his usual form of good nature, that of doing favour at other people's expense. His love of every gambling sport is notorious, and the sport of this district was cock fighting. Hardly a village hereabout but has its Cock Inn. The Cock Inn of Methwold stands at the extreme east end of the present street, and much of it is of Stuart date. The site of the old cock-pit may be just detected in the paddock behind it. In the days of Henri Quart's black-avised grandson, it was well outside of the village, and was the Rosherville of Methwold. The reputation of our gallic champions drew Charles over from Newmarket, and he dined at the Cock off Muel rabbits from his own manor, which proved much to his taste; and saw a main fought. Pleased with his entertainment, he granted Methwold a charter of arbitrary favoritism, which still lies in our church chest, by which we were relieved from sharing our neighbour's burdens in the way of tolls on roads and bridges. Our neighbours took their revenge for centuries by reporting that the king had found us too silly folk to bear the same charges as men of fuller intellect. Probably we gained in the end as little by his favour as we did by his personal example.

Yet, by his careless following out of his pleasures, Charles II. helped the growth of the democratic spirit. If Henry VIII. had played the Sultan in executing his wives, and raising his favourites from the ranks; if James I. had followed him in the latter particular; Charles II. had lifted Nell Gwynn from the pavement to the royal coach, and ennobled her offspring, and settled some of them hard by in Suffolk. Not even ability, merely animal charms could raise one now to easy association with royalty. Who of the lighter maidens of Methwold that he leered at beside the cock-pit might not rise by the same road? Vice could throw down all barriers, sport set all men on a level. Such was the lesson that Charles left by his visit to Methwold, probably, as by his general conduct elsewhere.

About this time small farming set in, and the houses of the smaller tenantry, many of which now form the most unsightly of our cottages, were growing up in our streets. They are constructed generally of heavy and rude wooden framework, the walls being filled in with chalk and a mortar that is almost innocent of lime. No touch of lingering taste characterizes them, and the Tudor buildings, that will survive them, present a significant contrast. Even in larger edifices, brick was giving way to wood and mortar. It was a ramshackle age.

CHAPTER VIII.

At the beginning of our Century.

THE state of Church affairs in Methwold at the beginning of this century reflects its condition throughout the country. It was the age of pluralities and non-residence. Not far off, in West Suffolk, five several incumbents hired one curate between them, of whom it is recorded that, getting a hint in the vestry one Sunday afternoon that woodcock had appeared in the neighbourhood, he ran to get his gun without doffing his canonicals. The incumbents themselves resided at Bath, Tunbridge Wells, London, or elsewhere. The Vicar of Methwold at that date was not singular in holding Cranwich and other parishes at the same time; but perhaps was to be commended for actually residing at Cranwich. For he was a man of family means, and the personal possessor of the great tithe of the parish. But in this he certainly was not to be praised, that, in 1800, when he took up his residence at Cranwich, having, I believe, previously lived in a hired house, perhaps the New Hall, at Methwold, he petitioned his Ordinary for leave to take up his abode at Cranwich, and stated in his petition, not only the fact that the vicarage here was unfit to reside in, but the untruth that the vicarial tithe, valued for commutation (as in all cases, no doubt, far below its value in kind) at £340, amounted to but £70 a year. It is significant of the condition of English consciences at the time, that he could procure three neighbours of condition to affix their signatures in support of this statement. I cannot discover how it was that the old vicarage house, as also a farm with woodland on the Brandon road, still called the Glebe, became alienated from the Church, but strange things were done in those days. Anyhow, the vicarage house since then has at one time served the purpose of a factory. For early in this century our villages were not without their local industries, which we now would so gladly restore, such as small factories contributory to Norwich or Sudbury, which were dotted everywhere about these counties. Next it served the far worse purpose of a local workhouse. And this brings us to speak of the terrible evils wrought in the villages by the iniquitous Enclosure Act, which was brought to bear on Methwold in 1807; evils which existed up to the time of passing the yet imperfect Poor Law Bill. This, for all its faults, as this was an open parish, did not here, as in many close parishes, entail the demolition of cottages, and the banishing of the labourers into the country towns, where the burgesses had to pay their poor rates, and whence they had to walk miles to and from their daily work.

The Enclosure Act, together with the disuse of local industries, left the labourer at the entire mercy of the employer. For the common-lands had enabled the labourer to possess a certain amount of property in the way of geese, young stock (locally known as buds), and milch kine, that gave him a measure of independence. Henceforward he had nothing to exist upon but his labour, and was virtually a slave, and unable to refuse any pittance that might be offered. The wage was thenceforward kept extremely low, and supplemented up to a point at which existence was just possible by a weekly dole of relief from the employers assembled in committee at the workhouse. The labourer became a weekly beggar.

The amount of this weekly dole was governed by the number of his household, whether adult or infant, and the birth of an illegitimate addition to his numbers was for the time absolutely welcome—in this way his daughters might bring grist to the mill—and our Church chests are still crowded with the bastardy orders of that time; whilst, to this day, the villagers have not recovered from the demoralizing effect of the careless morality so induced, and the mouths of parents or grandparents, so born, are closed against their ill-doing descendants.

And the Enclosure Act was framed on the principle

"to him that hath shall more be given"; the proprietors received shares of the common-land in proportion to what they already possessed. Only the most distant and unavailable portion of the common-land was reserved for the poor tenement holders, and divided to them in small rights, which at that distance they could not work to profit; whilst a temporary power of sale was added, which they naturally availed themselves of at any price, so as to make something of them for the moment. Meantime the larger landowners rounded off their farms with very considerable additions. In those days the following rude quatrain, not yet gone from the memory of the aged, was the popular song of Methwold—

> There was Dugmore for the College,
> And Bansbridge for the Crown;
> Houchen for old Newton,
> And the Devil for the Town.

The college or colleges, thus gibbetted justly, were Christ's and Sidney Sussex Colleges, at Cambridge, which had received from Henry VIII. the alienated lands of Brummel Priory here; Bansbridge was a leading official in the Duchy of Lancaster office; Houchen was a rising lawyer in the neighbourhood, who acted for William Newton, then owning the Hall Farm, a compact and valuable property, in the heart of the parish, to which the best part of the common adjoined; and it was no small feather in the lawyer's cap that he secured for his client a large slice of poor Tom Tiddler's ground, that abutted immediately on his estate. The devil, as usual, failed those who trusted him.

So the people, presently to be disgusted and impoverished by a corrupt Parliament, were deserted of their vicar in 1800, and left to the tender mercies of their employers without a spiritual consoler. For forty years of the century, the vicars of Methwold remained non-resident: then, at last, the present vicarage-house was built, not amidst the people—such contact was thought revolting—but at the furthest corner of a parish that extends to Southery, ten miles away; a little more, and it would have been clear of the parish altogether.

When, subsequently, pressure compelled the presence of a resident curate, he was, alas! a notorious drunkard, and his wife immoral also. Similar scandals also occurred in still later days, when his long reign of evil example had terminated. It is not to be wondered at therefore, that, by the thirties, Wesleyanism had become, and it remains, the established religion of Methwold; the people providing their own resident minister, who has a large chapel at Methwold, and a small affair at Otterings-hythe also.

Yet the vicar in 1800 was a pleasant and popular man. Religion was at a very low ebb, but the Church services, often but one a week in winter, were customarily well attended. He added to his popularity, it must be observed, by countenancing the prevalent lax observance of the Lord's Day. On that day it was usual to play a general game of camp-ball (football) in the Hall Close, and it was the custom of the genial parson, at the conclusion of afternoon service, to give the first kick, starting the ball from his raised position at the porch door, over the churchyard wall, then nearer than now.

The Lord's Day was the weekly holiday and only holiday of the labourer. Is it much more now? A quarter of a century ago, when curate-in-charge of the fen portion of Hilgay (Helingseye), men of middle age have told me how their cricket matches on Denver Green first began to be troubled by the drawing up on the neighbouring roadway of waggons loaded with local Wesleyan preachers and their voluntary choirs, who roared sermons against the desecration of the Sabbath, and hymns at intervals. And honesty obliges me sadly to confess that, whilst we have secured a religious observance of the labourer's holiday, we have sadly neglected the bodies and nerves of our poorer brethren in not simultaneously securing for them a half holiday for sport in the middle of the week. This omission on the part of the better off religious public has led, now that the labourer no longer shows himself at church to please the parson and his employer, to the miserable morning, with its unemployed lounging, and the subsequent resort to the public-houses, about which they gather an hour before the mid-day opening, which make the Sabbath too often a bad, exhausting, and demoralizing day of discontent to the labourer.

And the enclosers of the commons never thought

of leaving a Play-field for the labourer. Here, and in many other places, the manly and educative sport of cricket has died out for lack of ground to play on. The existence of a convenient piece of common made Denver a common resort for Sunday games after the enclosure had prohibited them elsewhere. We are obliged, as we look back to the earlier part of the century, to perceive that oligarchs are worse than tyrants, and that the grandfathers of our poor received less consideration from a parliament of country gentry, than from the older nobles and kings.

One exciting Sunday amusement remained for Methwold. They could fight, not one another, but the neigbouring villages; and very proud they were of their prowess. Methwold and Northwold were to each other as England and France, and some legacy of this sentiment remains. They met on the road between, or invaded each other's villages Sunday after Sunday. The son of a man not very long deceased has boasted that his father was more frequently carried home insensible from these encounters than any other man in Methwold. The fighting families are still recognized with a sort of honour.

I have noted how after the days of the Tudors, the main street of the village spread on, in inferior tenements, from the Fair Hill to the Cock Inn. To the south of this part of the street, in the crown of the wold, gaped the village chalk pit, the local quarry out of which most of the houses were built, and up to thirty years ago, two limekilns still smoked in its hollow.* But in 1812, the Duchy to whom the soil belongs, placed a school also in this hole, the first village school in Methwold. It was a poor structure of wood and chalk, built in two floors, the lower of which served for the teacher's residence, a man of very inferior attainments even in the matter of the "elements," whilst the upper, gained by an exterior ladder, was the school-room. To this charming site, down a hollow and miry pathway overhung by thorn and bramble, the village children made their way for their daily "larning," till the private efforts of a young and vigorous schoolmaster from a distance, who had a desire for a decent home to bring "his girl" to, presently contrived, after securing the aid of the tenantry in the way of gratuitous carriage of materials, to induce the Duchy of Lancaster to build the fine room and convenient residence which form the nucleus of the present excellent schools on the Bone Close.

Before closing this chapter, I would for a moment turn attention to the fen. In 1785 an Act had been passed to encourage the home growth of hemp, then as since mainly imported from Russia, and each parish was expected to produce its quota. There was a low islet, of very fair soil, which lay just outside Katsholme to the west, and this was given up to the growth of the plant. Although this attempt

---

* These limekilns, before they became extinct, had become gruesome to the surrounding cottages, through a lime-burner having been crushed by a fall of the chalk, and uttering such groans in his expiring agonies as caught his wife's ear in one of the cottages a hundred yards away, but too late for his safe release.

to keep out the foreigner was abandoned early in the century, a cottage that for a time was weighted with an upper storey, since removed as liable to sink it in the unsteady soil, still stands there; and the almost imperceptible rise is still called the Hempplash, or Hemplash. The meaning of the suffix I have tried in vain to unravel, perhaps my readers may be more successful.

Looking back at the days of my youth and at the Chartist and other movements, and thinking of the Reform Bill and the intense opposition it evoked from the gentry, in the light of things recorded in this chapter, one can but feel that the country, early in this century, passed through a worse time than she had known from the times of the early Plantagenets, and, thank God, that we have got so far as we have on the road of improvement without a revolution, and that no Kett of later days led the people of Norfolk to civil bloodshed.

CHAPTER IX.

In my own Days.

I HAVE had nineteen years' acquaintance with Methwold. I feel at home in Norfolk, for my grandfather hailed from New Buckenham, and my great grandmother from Norwich. One Richard Gegge,* a reputed forbear, centuries ago held Buckenham and Tofts, and Ickburgh hard by; two centuries earlier the Gegges are said to have reigned at Oxburgh. Anyhow, I find the people congenial to my nature.

---

* Mr. Coulton has, I think, recently explained "Gay" as signifying "track," and Gedge or Gegge as "ford." Is not "gay" rather connected with the French *gué*, ford? Gedge is usually interpreted as coming from the token or crest of the family, which some of the Gages also, I think, have borne, and signifying luce, pike. This word would then be connected with gudgeon, as don (fort) with donjon, and pie, pica, pike (mottled) with pigeon. It is just possible that the term "jack" for pike is connected with the same root in some such form as gedgic, little gegh; gegh being the oldest writing of the name. I do not think that the giving of surnames from localities ever originated at a very early date. The Gays, for instance, would have taken their surname probably since Norman times, as the Oxburghs, Metholds, Gayfords, and hosts of others.

The establishment of Wesleyanism here, sadly easily accounted for, is distressful to a clergyman, but the free and independent spirit of the place tries me less than it would many. Mine have been days of calamity for the farmer, and I have wondered at the courage with which it has been borne. The country lawyer, in this no wiser than the rest, had been the general adviser; yeomen had bought the lands, half on mortgage, at twice their present value, at his suggestion, and borrowed additional sums to work them; now they have with difficulty "got out of them," at prices which have barely recouped the mortgagees; and become penniless, falling to the condition of labourers, or securing work as stewards and such like elsewhere. Their fathers dying nominally possessed of considerable estates, left ruin, instead of competence to their children; the son who took the management, often the possession by purchase, of his brothers' and sisters' share of the family lands, being the chief victim. The management of such a parish is an impossible task for a clergyman, unless he be possessed of a fortune, and prepared to spend it. To work so extended a district, a mission hall at Otteringhythe, and another by Powplot, where the population has increased with the construction, or rather the improving, under Judges' order, of the road between Feltwell and Southery, would be absolutely necessary. Before this, and the Duchy road through the centre of the fen, were made, I kept touch with that part of the parish by a cottage lecture, to which I made my way over lands and across ditches with a lantern strapped to my waist, on Wednesday evenings, through snow and storm, without fail, in winter; and by a service in a barn seven miles away on Sunday evenings in summer. Now the fen folk prefer to take the road to Southery or Feltwell for association with their kind on Sundays, and such efforts have been for some years abandoned as unacceptable.

The vicarial tithe, now very much reduced, and unusually drawn upon by the exigencies of a place that contains no wealthy residents, will not support a curate, or indeed afford me an income equal to that I once enjoyed as a curate. But my relations with the people are quite as pleasant as I could expect, and I have effected something as a minister and a citizen. The Church has been re-warmed and lighted. The porch, still used as a vestry, is no longer a cause of death to the ratepayers, the windows having been glazed, and suitable doors placed where only a kind of half-door existed at my coming. A lectern in iron and wood, constructed for me by my sexton and his cousin,—my sexton made the simple lamp standards also from my design—forms an ornament of the nave. The churchyard, till then a neglected field, crossed only by one public roadway, has been laid out with paths that render it everywhere available, and which are pleasant strolling places in summer. Graves are attended to, and rough mounds replaced by well-kept flower beds in many instances. The church fabric has been kept in repair, and the east end improved. The village streets have been lighted, which fact has added much to nightly decorum as well as convenience. I have spoken before of the raising of the settlement-stone and marking it again with a cross, and of the restoration of the Clifton brass. I have taken a town-clerk's place in parish business of all sorts: my parish correspondence fills several drawers. Music has received constant attention,—not only church music,—for singing classes for concerted music have hardly ever been wanting during our régime, and several cantatas have been executed by our local chorus. The coal club, re-arranged, provides some sixty of the poorest householders with coal, served out weekly under my own eye, for fifteen weeks of the winter at under 7*d.* the cwt., the tenantry helping me by contributing free cartage from the railway, and acting as a general committee. There is an equally large clothing club; a small shoe club, and a penny bank. The hour of vestry meetings has been changed; a concession to the poorer ratepayers which I hope they will yet acknowledge, to their own honour, by still further improving their behaviour, which is already growing more dignified. For the encouragement of others who, like myself, have to be perpetual prime-ministers to their community, I think I ought to give the results of this change thus far. When I, with many secret fears, and amidst many heart-burnings, stood staunch for the holding of parish meetings at the time convenient for the labourer, I had two excellent churchwardens, for both of

P

whom I had a strong personal affection; the one, a strong Churchman and a Conservative, was utterly opposed; the other, a Conservative but hardly a Churchman, was so bitter against the change that he never forgave it to the day of his much-lamented decease. It could be truly affirmed that, so long as he was not accommodated, there was nothing hopeful in the temper or attitude of the labourer. So discouraging, too, were the first results of the change, that a friend at Southery, one of my colleagues on the school board, who has also land and a place on vestry meetings in Methwold, himself a Liberal and a Dissenter, rarely loses an opportunity of expressing to me his scornful opinion of the Methwold labourer. But I believe in the good sense of humanity as a whole, when they come under the correction of experience, and the ennobling effects of confidence; still more in the good sense of Englishmen; and most of all in the good hearts of my own people. So I held fast in silence, though within I suffered much; and not the less, as may be imagined, because my own special churchwarden and friend to this day absents himself, when possible, from parish meetings. But what is the fact? Already the conduct of the labourers, who attend in large numbers, has become such as is worthy of Englishmen, and contrasts, greatly to their advantage, with what we read of the vestry meetings of small bodies of wealthy metropolitans. The most cantankerous (and these are not necessarily of the labouring class), if they put a little that is grating into their voice and attitude, have ceased to be angry and rude, with that rudeness which comes of having an evident grievance. Where they are, or think they are, subject to wrong under the present condition of the laws regarding the choice of parish officers, they are content to protest and to signify their desire for change; and the whole community has, by force of contact, been brought to acquire a *modus vivendi* amongst themselves in public life. Things are not perfect, nor ever will be; but anyhow the masses no longer stand angrily apart from us, nursing evil and degrading sentiments, because they are treated as naughty children, unworthy to be invited to take a part in the state. Methwold has taken a step forward in charity, in common life, and mutual family feeling. The masses are being levelled up instead of being held aside and kept down. I have myself had occasion to employ one of the bitterest agitators of past times, who probably will yet again and again show his suspiciousness and irritability. I have watched him narrowly. I find him a man of distinctly superior intelligence and activity: one who was sure to form opinions, and vehemently uphold them by what he thought he saw and heard. The only cure for such is fuller information, practical experience and responsibility, and the power of expressing, without hindrance, for correction or acceptance, his own thoughts on things. Such men may be made very useful in the mass; whilst, if left to conduct a guerilla warfare from the outside, they are a lifelong torment to the community;

and, in closely-governed communities they obtain an influence which is dangerous, and a character which tends still to deteriorate and to further embitter their behaviour, such as they would not obtain under more charitable and generous treatment. There is a family feeling about the place, and the vicarage is not outside the family. We gather many of our neighbours in weekly "At Homes," now at the vicarage, now in the farm-houses of the parish, in the winter, and enjoy each other's society thoroughly. Our young people have their fêtes in summer, and school-room parties in the winter, at which dancing, the only refined game for the united sexes, is welcomed, and not abused in any way. We hope religion has not gone back: we know that civilization and manners have greatly gone forward. In fact, we have done what seemed possible for us—we, for my family has done at least as much of the work as myself.

The school-room has become a polling place, and a frequent centre for political meetings of both parties. These meetings, the labourers and their families flock to, treating them as interesting lectures, and they behave excellently; whilst the speakers of either party generally pay them the compliment of treating them as worthy of careful reasoning. Personal abuse of opponents is not at all approved of by a Methwold audience.

A large Public Hall has now been added to the possessions of Methwold, standing in the ground where the Tudor house near the George Inn, figured

amidst the relics of the Tudor period, used to stand. It will be named after the patron saint of the parish, and, like the centre of town life in mighty Liverpool, be known as the "St. George's Hall." For this we are indebted to the exertions of the promoter of the fruit colony, who has displayed astonishing nerve and perseverance in soliciting subscriptions from the liberally-disposed throughout the country, to enable him to present his native place with an advantage that our own resources could never have secured. Every considerable village should have its public hall; for a public room is an incitement to public efforts after social improvement, to reading, to lectures, to parish bands and musical societies, to athletic clubs, to dancing classes even, which have their proper place in civilization, and to many other attempts which, if they have but temporary or alternating success, all help towards social life and mutual interest amongst the various classes of a community. As the Americans build railways that population may follow, so it is a gain where social institutions find in their midst a home waiting to receive them. These "homes of the community" have a place, by way of a witness and an appeal, which comes only after the "houses of God in the land."

Education has of course advanced. At the time of my in-coming, the schools had just been handed over, from the proprietorship of the Queen, to the management of the vicar and churchwardens. The zealous master, who had ensured the erection of the new school-room, remains to this day under the new system. The expenditure on the school in 1882 had been £114; in 1891 it had reached £322. Yet, to this hour, a yearly contribution of £80 from the Duchy, combined with the fees and the grant, have supported both the great schools here, and a dependent school at Otteringhythe; and rarely left any margin to be paid by the parishioners. For a large number of fen children, we are contributory to the board schools at Southery; and on that board I sit now as a member. I found an infant school in the course of erection to the rear of the large school-room here: since then I have been my own architect; and the building of classrooms, of new offices of all sorts, of an addition to the master's house, and of vestibules both to the infants' and the mixed schools, and of the school at Hythe, have been well and economically effected; so well, indeed, that our schools have been cited as a model. The schools are classed "excellent," and have a name in the district. The addition of drawing to the curriculum has obliged me, *faute de meilleur*, to undertake gratuitously the drawing instruction.

At Southery we have singular difficulties to contend with, the fen population being recruited from the failures on the high land, and somewhat migratory, and many residing without the school radius. Also the difficulty of inuring the young sufficently early to agricultural labour, so that they may not resent its loneliness and roughness in fenny localities, as they do if brought to it later, and resolve to quit the country for the towns (often to their own material disadvantage) at the first chance of an opportunity of escape, renders managers, who have a fen population to deal with, unwilling to enforce full attendance beyond the third standard; which militates against educational proficiency. The Southery schools have, in consequence, never become "excellent," and I find myself obliged to give in somewhat to the exigencies of the locality. Moreover, there is this disadvantage to board schools in an open parish, that the members of the board, as a body, are not of a class that can afford much time for personal attention to the working of the schools under their charge. In fact, for such schools, a visitor, in addition to the inspector, who only examines, or visits very occasionally, ought to be appointed in each division of the county.

Our earliest attempts to establish the classes supplied by the Technical Education Committee of the County Council, as well as a previous long and persevering attempt, through ten years, to draw the labouring classes to make use of a reading-room, proved that at present such things were attractive, with rare exceptions, to the artizan class only; but it is through the example of this class, out of which our choirs and our disciples in culture are mainly drawn, that we must work, to overcome, by an example that already touches some few, the hereditary influence of habit amongst those whose forefathers have lived a hand-to-mouth life, without thought or enterprize; and the second year's efforts have been much more hopeful, as regards the labouring class, than those of the first year. Lectures on home nursing were attended throughout by an average of over ninety females, and really earnest interest excited. Much was learned that will never be forgotten, and a desire to add to the acquirements of the housemother, in the way of usefulness and nicety, was awakened in many gentle hearts, that only needed the instruction—not the inclination—to be all they could to their homes.

The labouring class, almost exclusively, furnished two large classes for drawing and carpentry, which included men with families of their own, who addressed themselves to their subject with all the seriousness of their age and experience. "I never thought to have come to this in my time," said one of these, by no means one of the most successful, as he contemplated with just satisfaction the laborious results of his endeavour to draw to scale a glazed door with all its panels, tenons, and the rest, tolerably correctly set down on paper. The younger members bid fair now to "come to this" and much more in their time; and it was with just self-congratulation that we sent up some forty money boxes, and the drawings of them in elevation, plan, and section, to the General Secretary at Norwich, in the middle of our second year's session.

The full contact between the educated classes and the labourer is not yet established. He resents the old patronage; we have not yet found the way to a mutual understanding. His education is too much, as yet, of forcework to be attractive. As yet we cannot inoculate him with our interests, and he does not enter into our tastes. In course of time education, more prudently applied—for the elementary education system of the country is, as yet, doctrinaire rather than practical—will do something; a share in parish business will do something; but it must be a work of time and patience; we must associate ourselves freely with any of them that show an inkling of our wider perceptions, and trust through these to understand and be understood of the masses. The Church clergy feel deeply the mutual distance. The labourer does not appreciate the Church Service; and the dissenting chapels in the country leave no place for the mission chapels of the towns, with their more congenial services. Is there a possible hint in his interest in political discussion? If the body of the Church could, on the Sunday afternoons, be open for religious discussions; liberty of-speech, within proper limits, and under the rule of the clergyman, being granted, and questions allowed; might we in this way come to know and respect each other? At present, we can rarely get close to each other, save in the hour of sorrow. We want to know the poor man as a brother; not to be tolerated or even admired of him; and this is hard to attain, much harder in dealing with a Teutonic race, than with one of Latin origin, where class separation is less instinctive; or a Celtic people, amongst whom certain common elegancies of taste are universal. How to level up in tastes and sympathies is the question for the nation. At present we fear there is more thought of solving the difficulty by levelling down, and the low and high know each other best when what is called "sport" is in question.

How little do we know of what moves in their minds. Strange beliefs linger amongst them, beliefs older than history. When our English Solomon took pattern from Saul in starting a witch-hunt, he did not know he was simply coming on a yet lingering heathenism, remnants of British magic and such like, which he was foolish enough to treat seriously. Some of them still linger. Here is a specimen. A wiry, ascetic-looking, but far from ascetic-living, man, who died a few years since, was employed in leading a cart-stallion of very uncertain temper. Yet he would lie by the roadside to sleep off a booze, keeping hold of the leading rein, without fear, and actually without suffering. Why? Because he trusted in a charm. In a small box of silver—let Mr. Rudyard Kipling note this—he carried a certain bone of a frog—the tongue bone probably—secured in this wise.

On St. Mark's eve, that is, at the end of the Fair, and about the time of the old Fire-festival, having previously captured a frog, and placed it in a "pismires' hill" till it was reduced to a skeleton, let one gather the bones, and carry them to running water, no man observing. There let him cast them in, and one small bone will rise and float against the current. This is the charm. But how shall he have light for the experiment? Because there will be one, whom we name not, at hand to give him light. So, too, fern seed—brake seed they call it—is gathered by some on the same night. The fern-leaves themselves shall shine to light the seeker. These, too, must be placed in a box of silver, or they fail of force. By help of these one man could tend his horses in the dark, where others needed a lantern; another could drive a loaded wain across the fen lands, where no other could drive one empty.

When talking of superstitions, we may add a ghost story, told to me first-hand. The scene is the road between the Vicarage and the Wents. On a starlight night in December, 1892, a working engineer's wife, of some twenty-nine years, having particular occasion to report herself to the doctor at Northwold, was walking thither between a female married friend on the left, and her husband on the right; on the left-hand side of the road. When nearing Pottisford Run, the friend remarked, "they say there is something to be seen here; perhaps we shall meet that which frightened that bad old"—mentioning a character whose domestic reputation had not been of the best. The expectant mother answered with a refusal to believe in any such things, and a jeer at such as did. After crossing the Run, and coming to where, half way between it and the Vents Farm, the hedge is high and unbroken, the women both perceived (so my first informant said) a man in dark clothes, with no hat on, coming on their side of the road, at a very rapid pace: he was about twenty yards distant when first seen. He came up with no hint of turning aside; and the scoffer had no thought of anything odd, but somehow felt shamefaced at staring at a man without his hat, so can give no account of his face. A moment, and he seemed as if he would thrust the other woman aside from the hedge, and she screamed, fearing he was about to lay hands on her; but, instead, he passed off at right angles through the high hedge, with a sound as of a wind blast, or of scratching garments. The frightened friend fell so heavily on the neck of my informant, that she fell against her husband, knocking him out into the road. He, recovering himself, asked what that noise had been in the hedge, but averred that he had not seen the man. The subsequent consequences on the woman's health were disastrous. An after interview with the second woman elicited the following, even more uncanny, variation:—"She is wrong, I did not see it coming, I felt it all in a moment; it seemed to be trying to get a hold of me, that's why I screamed so. I could not see, but I could hear it go, just the same as she did."

Cautious enquiry elsewhere resulted in the statement, that "So-and-so had once seen ' *its* ' face; '*it*' was old R——, 'the bad old fellow,' who lived in such a house in the street (a great-nephew till lately dwelt on the site), who owned the grass piece close by that side of the run (*i.e.*, stream)."

Where the evidence of three senses, seeing, feeling, and hearing, is supposed to be producible, it is not likely that it will affect much to laugh at credulity in the above case. Such things are still talked, and I fancy believed, side by side with the mysteries of Christianity. The cross is yet planted in the magic stone of eld; some roots of religion still reach back amidst superstitions of the devil; these are plants yet to be rooted up.

Still more recently, the above has received an additional touch of confirmation from a most unexpected quarter. Tempted by the curiosity of a gentleman who had visited us at all hours from a neighbouring parish, to think there was something at the bottom of his questions, we were incited to ask if he had ever seen anything himself, before we recited our tale. With some hesitation he replied, "No, I have seen nothing, but I have *felt* something. It was very queer, it was something rushing that touched me." After this we told him the story, and he shook his head over it.

One turns again, with something of relief, to things material. Let us take a final survey of the present village. The High Street extends now from the Cock Inn westward and downward, with various curves after it has passed the George Inn, past the church, the Hall Close, the Cross Hill, and the Bone Close to the Pits Corner westward; a further continuation still bears the name of Buntings. Where the George stands, islanded between two narrow ways, two foldgates or fallgates probably stood in Tudor times; later the foldgate here was moved a hundred yards to the east, and a fragment of stonework with a mass of rubble attached that once belonged to it lies in a neighbouring yard. Just outside this folgate rose later a rival hostelry with accommodation lands for stock, now used for the weekly market, and for the Stock Fair on St. George's Day; but the Pleasure Fair, as well as the ghost of the old Statute Fair at Michaelmas (in common speech, the Stattis or Statters) which was the fair for annual hiring of hinds and servant maids, are held on the Fair Hill. The narrow entrance from Feltwell, near the Cross Hill, is still called the Folgate. In the old farm-house hard by, now divided into four cottages, two of which serve as lodgings for tramps; a flourishing boarding-school for farmers' daughters was kept early in the century. Close by, the son of a local wheelwright, who made his fortune in business at Adelaide (South Australia) has erected a line of alms-houses, in concrete with zinc roofs, after the fashion of the land of his adoption.

The folgates remind us of the days when the land was guiltless of hedgerows. Then the cattle were driven by day, under charge of the children or aged, to feed on the "mere baulks" which divided the patches of corn-land, or on the neighbouring pastures, and folded by night in the villages. The town bull roared outside the windows, and served for contumelious comparison with roaring children.

The Statute Fair reminds us how young men, as well as young women, resided for the year in the farm-houses, and fed together in the large kitchens.* A sort of family connection was thus established between employer and employed, which had its value. They stand now only on business relations, and nothing short of an actual community of business interest will again closely connect them. Independent, but with little but his labour to depend on, the labourer has now an anomalous position, and Unionism cannot much help him. We doubt if on the whole it does much for the town worker—co-operation would certainly do more. Migration and emigration tempt the labourer, but he often finds his way back, for the gain of a change of locality is often, save to the energetic few, imaginary rather than real. Yet we have colonies at Bolton in Lancashire, and at Ypsilanti in Michigan, where Methwold families have gathered their relations

---

* There is abundant evidence that the habit of domiciling the boys and youths in the farm-houses, gave scope for many abuses that tended to produce hereditary distrust, and to make the labourer turn his back on his master's interests, once he became thoroughly independent. Although there were some farms where the treatment of the dependant was humane, and even generous, especially in the harvest season; there were others in which merciless whippings by an irresponsible tyrant, fireless back kitchens, from which the only refuge was a shivering couch in an unfurnished garret, resorted to so soon as the supper could be hurried down; and a general treatment that was unsympathetic and degrading, left a life-long resentment in the hearts of the poor, the memory of which has by no means passed away. And perhaps it may be too true that the country parson cared too much to be on terms with his tithe-payer to pose as the friend of the helpless in such cases; and so has also brought on his successors some share of this hereditary lack of confidence on the part of the labouring class. Paternal relations on the part of one class towards another produce ever very evil fruits, if these older children be neglected or unconsidered, or in any way exploited for the advantage of the superior class. Perhaps, considering what human nature is, it is better that such relations should only exist where they are safeguarded by natural affection.

to them; and innumerable settlers elsewhere in America, Africa, and Australasia. It is touching to mark on the cottage walls, galleries of small photographs, by which some aged granddame fancies she knows relatives she has never seen, or will never again see in the flesh.

Neither the Army nor Navy have much attraction here. The discharged soldier or reserve man is an unsettled being when he comes back to his village, and it is not thought that "much good is got of soldiering." The tramps' lodging-house, too, receives too many that have passed the ranks, amongst its inmates. The uniform most aimed at is that of the railway porter; his work is well paid, and the life is fairly independent. The majority of the young girls pass their later years of service in the large towns; some marry away, all come back for their holidays with a well-dressed appearance and a more modish air. It is strange that so many of them as do should settle down to a cottage life in the old place after all, but even abroad they many of them mate to other emigrants from the old village home.

Talking of the labourer, I cannot express the result of long experience better than by the following extract from a letter I had occasion to write to the Organizing Secretary of Technical Education at Norwich, early in the present year (1893):—

"The Home Nursing Lectures are, at present, extremely popular, drawing an attendance of some eighty females; and may continue to do so, as they last but through some five weeks, and require no effort, save a willingness to be instructively entertained.

"The Drawing and Carpentry Lectures, on the contrary, are as much more an anxiety to us this year, and require as much more effort to prevent their ending in entire failure, with consequent money loss to a community unable and unprepared to meet it, as the labouring class, out of which the two classes this year are mainly formed, is less dependable than the artisan and tradesman class, out of which our one class was taken last year. An examination of our lists proves that the most regular attendants, thus far, are the few that stand in some degree removed from the general conditions of the labouring class, or the elder men who have chosen to join.

"Thus far the labourer, poor dear fellow, is in many of his characteristics a child. He sticks to nothing, he recognizes no claim upon his patience. I have proved this, more especially during my score of years in this parish, by night school, reading, concert, cantata, lecture, and lastly by these technical classes. That which inevitably, in the end, raises and distinguishes individuals, classes, and races, is the acquired habit of tenacity, the preserving power of patience. In this place you see the labourer at his simplest, in an open and Dissenting parish. He is nearly as free as a child from malice; but he is as bare of formed principles and habits of discipline. Here he is afraid of no man, and there is little whereby to bribe him. Perhaps, like the child, he needs more of the rod and of the sugar-plum to hold him for a time to any line of action for his own good. He gives his word lightly, and as lightly breaks it. His predominant form of religious profession here perhaps touches him more easily, as it accommodates itself more to his untrained instincts, but it does less to raise him in the scale of social being. One can forgive him much, perhaps everything, but one wishes very much more for him. How to hold him to anything, till one has effected any definite advance, is the great, and hitherto unsolved difficulty. Our present utterly vicious school system, under which no child is left by patient assiduity to discover the way of acquiring perfectly any lesson for himself, but is entirely spoon-fed and crammed to disgust by the master, is doing less than nothing to awaken intelligence in the labouring class. It is destroying his initiative, and rendering him more bare of self-help than ever."

Those of our emigrants who have really done well abroad have been largely of the artizan class. The connection maintained between the home depôt and our relatives abroad is constant. Intermarriage has been a cause of close union and much clannishness, and I think I could tell a Methwold girl anywhere by her free gait. Foreigners, even from the neighbouring parishes, are coldly esteemed, and a "foreign" origin is remembered for generations. The cottage home is rarely neglected; the sitting-room is generally bright; the bed-room has its petticoated toilet table, its table ornaments, and its neat side carpets, even where the occupant is of the poorest. And the people are nice feeders, with a strong preference for butcher's meat over pork. Turf is discarded for coal, as untidy, except on the scullery hearth. In such matters the change has been rapid, for I have heard a farmer tell of the day, as a day of wonder, when the first hundred-weight of coal was deposited in his father's "lodge;" and the consumption of pork was once so universal that no other viand was known as "meat." Brick floors are confined to the older cottages; carpets have entirely replaced sand; the smock is only worn by a few shepherds, whereas fifty years ago even the farmer wore a white smock on Sunday. A considerable number of shops has ousted the hawker and the Scotchman. No longer does the farmer's wife lay in a stock of dress pieces bought for fancy of the travelling dealer, perhaps never to be made up. Things are bought when wanted, and according to fashion too. In a word, the place is by no means old fashioned or out of the world.

In one thing it has retrograded greatly, as I fear have a vast number of our villages, namely, in the matter of dairy produce. The little farm-house servant now kept is unable, and the farmer's wife unwilling, to make butter such as comes from Dane and Breton. Before the enclosure, say the aged, there were sixty cows on the common; now none are possessed by the labouring class, and fewer cows are kept on the farms. It is greatly to be desired that technical classes and dairy exhibitions may give a fresh start to this, the most profitable branch of farming in our counties.

The labourer and his family read largely on a Sunday. His literature is really enormous in the way of newspapers and periodicals. The press has a vast responsibility in the formation of his character, and as yet we fear he reads too much of party virulence and of police reports, whilst his religious journals are spiced with too much bitterness, and strange, irregular ideas. One of the most favourite of their religious journals goes in largely for Millenarious fancies, contemporary prophecy, and such like "cranks." Should we ever attain a mid-week half holiday, it would be well to publish secular journals of a high character, yet suited to his taste, on the Tuesday rather than on the Saturday. Here would be a great opening for really patriotic, and not party, authors of instruction.

The nomenclature of the parish, homogeneous as we are, proves our very various origin in the past. We have our local names, such as Wortley (cabbage field), Flatt (of the fen), Cock (of the Inn of that sign), our Lawes (Saxon, meadows), our Fendycks (Dutch, Vandijk), our Goodriches (Goodric), who gave their name to neighbouring Gooderston (Godric's ton), for as Norwic was sounded Norwich, and bric, bridge; so was Ethelric sounded Etheridge, and Godric, Goodrich. We have Norman Thibaults, generally written Tibbett or Tebbut; we have Danish Boldrys, we have Mediæval Armigers, and Scotch Gordons, and so on. But the locality has assimilated them all, and the general resemblance is strong. In a word, the people have a character and appearance of their own, by which they may be known, appreciated, and, to my thinking at least, loved. I have found pleasure in residing amongst them; and, if Providence ever remove me elsewhere, shall remember them with regret, and never lose the sense of belonging to them.

In writing my small history of the locality, I feel that I have written much of the history of the nation, but with a difference that is all its own;

> Still lies each village camped a tribe apart
> Upon its lands and individual,
> Where, as in households, each need fill the part
> God gave him, to make sure the wealth of all:
> Not, as the lost in some vast capital,
> Feel we no touch with all that next us lies,
> But each one's joy or sorrow is a call
> For common thrill, and kindred sympathies;
> And our own microcosm still supplies
> Enough to make us more than a mere name;
> And he who served his generation dies
> Sure of just memory, though he knows not fame,
> And may be numbered with the truly great,
> The more, that he contemned not his small state.

INDEX.

A.

Absenteeism, effects of, 44

Alms-houses, Coote's, 118

Acts or Laws for—Removal of Markets, 39; Enclosure, 94-96; Hemp Growing, 100, 101; Poor Relief, 94-96

Amusements, deterioration of popular, 74, 75

Architecture—
(a) *Domestic*—British, 9; Roman, 5, 18, 19; Saxon, 23; Norman and Plantagenet, 34, 35; Tudor, the Vicarage, 66-68, 94; the New Hall, 60, 75, 76; the De Mundeford House, 70, 73; the Clifton House (?), 77, 78; other Tudor work, 72, 73; Jacobean, 49, 50, 91

(b) *Ecclesiastical*—Church at Buntings, 24-26; Church at Ottering-hythe, 27; St. George's Church, 38-46, 62

Architecture, effects on taste of, 47

Architect, acting as one's own, 110

B.

Bats, cutting willows for, 15

Bible, effects on nation of publishing, 60, 61

Bone Close, the, 7, 9, 100, 117

Brass, the De Clifton (mis-written Clifford on illustration), 51-57

Brickwork—Specimens of the Old Vicarage, 65-67; De Mundeford House, 71; Old Gable, 73

British Times, in, Chapter I., 1-12

British Settlement, the first, 5-10

Brummel (or Broom-hill), Priory of, 4, 27, 83, 96

Buildings, for the various, described. See Architecture

Buntings, Saxon village of, 23, 24, 117

Buntings, traces of Church of, 24-26

Burning alive of an aged couple, 69, 70

C.

Carving—
(a) In stone:—From older Church, 25; Market Cross, 36, 37; in St. George's Church, 45, 46; Chimney Piece, 77

(b) In wood:—Church Roof, 48; Work in Old Vicarage, 66, 67; Jacobean Cradle, 69, 79 (illus-

tration); Tudor Bedstead, 69; Hearth Curbs, 72, 77
Catsham. See Katsholm
Century, at the beginning of our, Chapter VIII., 93-124
Chalk Pit, the, 99, 100
Charter given by Charles II., 91
Characteristics of Methwold, 43, 53, 62, 82, 91, 95, 96
Chests in Church, 52
Churches of Buntings, Methwold, Hythe. See Architecture
Clergy, celibacy of, 26
Clogs, cutting soles for, 15
Cock Inn, the, 90, 117
Coffins, stone, 28
Common Lands, 88
Cornholm, 22
Cottages, decency of interiors of, 122
Cradle, oaken, of 1660. See Carving
Crosses, 5, 6, 37
Cross Hill, the, 5, 7, 117

D.
Dairy farming, 123
Drainage of Fens, &c.—Roman, 15-18, 22, 84; Mediæval, 85, 86; Stuart, 16, 82-90
Dress, abandonment of older, 122
Drown, the great, 89
Drying up of streams, &c., 2, 16, 17

E.
Earthworks, 29
Ecclesiastical art, educational influence of, 47
Education—*Schools*, 7, 100, 109, 110; *Technical classes*, 110, 112, 120, 121
Eldern's (Ealdorman's) Lane, 4, 24
Emigration and Migration, 119, 120

F.
Fair, the St. George's, 10, 11, 28, 36, 37, 70, 74, 75; the Statute or Statters, 118
Fair-ground and Fair Hill, 26, 36, 40, 60, 70
Farmers, ruin of, 103
Fen lands of Methwold, 82-90
Folgates (Fold or Fall-gates), 117, 118
Franck, Anthony, Vicar. See Persons

G.
Ghost-story, 115-117
Grenaker, 5
Grims-dyke, Grimshoe, Grimes-graves, 17
Guilds, 47, 62-64

H.
Haggard or Hoggard. See Persons
Hall, the St. George's, 108, 109
Hall-close, the, 34, 39, 75, 77
Hall, the de Warennes', 34-36
Hall Farm, the, 2, 4, 24, 96
Half-holiday, call for, in the country, 98, 123
Hangings, the, 83
Hardes, fords, 87
Harst-holme or Harvest-holme, 22
Hemplash, 100
Houses, various, described. See Architecture
Huns (Hern-lands), 15
Humble pit (Holmebrig pit), 14
Hythe, the. See Ottering-hythe

I.
Inundations of Fen, 86, 89
Innums or Inholmes, 22

K.

Kings of England referred to. See Persons
Kats-holme (St. Catherine's-holme), 22, 23, 27, 84, 100

L.

Labourers, present attitude of, 112, 113
Labourers, domiciled on farms, 119
Lancaster, House of, its relations to the Crown, 63
Level, alterations of, in Fen, 84, 85
Literature of the labourer, 113
Longevity in the Fens, 76

M.

Mundefords, the De. See Persons
Mundeford's, De, the town house of. See Architecture
Muel, 32, 33
Manby, Rear-Admiral. See Persons

N.

Names altered by assimilation, 3, 4, 7, 23
New Hall, the, 75, 76
Norfolk dialect, 9
Norman days, in, Chapter IV., 32-37

O.

Olave's-holme, St. See Slusham
Ottering-hythe, the, 3, 5, 23, 28, 83, 88, 103, 110

P.

Pagan-incomers, times of the, Chapter III., 21-31

Parish efforts and institutions, 104, 105, &c.
Peltry-market, 36
Persons referred to, names of, &c.—
    Armiger, 123
    Ayloff, Sir W., 87
    Anthony, Thomas, 87
    Bansbridge, 96
    Blomefield, 54
    Boldry, 123
    Brandon, Charles, 71
    Charles I., 49, 53, 81, 88
    Charles II., 90
    Cliftons, the De, 51, 52, 77, 78
    Cromwell, 53, 86, 89
    Coulton, Mr. J. J., 77, 83
    Dugmore, 96
    Edward I., 43, 86
    Edward III., 39
    Edward IV., 46
    Elizabeth, 68, 79
    Etheridge (Ethelric), 9, 124
    Franck, Rev. Anthony, 52, 53
    Fludyck, 123
    Flatt, 123
    Gedge, 102
    Grinling, Gibbons, 48
    Gloucester, Duke of, 46
    Goodrich, 9, 123, 124
    Gordon, 123
    Greenwell, Canon, 17
    Haggard or Hoggard, 14
    Henry VI., 46
    Henry VII., 58, 68
    Henry VIII., 59, 71, 91, 96
    Henri Quart, 8
    James I., 80, 81, 87, 91
    James II., 53
    Lancaster, Dukes of, 63

Persons referred to, names of, &c.—
  Laud, 64
  Leicester, Earl of, 27
  Manby, Admiral, 76
  Margaret (Queen), 46
  Mundeford, De, 35, 60, 65, 70-73, 76, 87
  Newton, 96
  Popham (Lord), 86
  Richard II., 63, 86
  Sams, Dr., 17, 84
  Stewart, Elizabeth, 86, 89
  Swift, Thos., 52-54
  Tibbett or Tebbutt, 123
  Vermuyden, Sir Cornelius, 88, 89
  Warenne, De, Earl, 24, 26, 27, 32, 33, 34, 43
  Wortley, 123
  Younge or Young, 52, 53, 88, 89
Pit, the. See Chalk-pit
Pits-corner or Pitch-corner, 3
Places referred to—
  Adelaide, 18
  Arques, 8
  Beechamwell, 17
  Brancaster, 5, 22
  Brandon, 5, 18, 37
  Bolton, 119
  Bruges, 42
  Bury St. Edmund's, 16, 46
  Burnt-fen, 7
  Castle-acre, 8, 18, 27, 29
  Castle Rising, 31
  Cranwich, 17, 93, 94
  Dereham, 23
  Denver, 86, 88, 98, 99
  Ely, 41
  Erith, 86, 88

Places referred to—
  Feltwell, 5, 13, 17, 71, 83, 84, 103, 104
  Fordham, 23, 84, 87
  Fincham, 41
  Haberdon (or Aber-don, water fort), near Bury St. Edmund's, 16, 63
  Hilgay, 3, 23, 83, 87, 98
  Ickburgh, 18, 102
  Ickworth, 16
  Lakenheath, 89
  Littleport, 85
  Lynn Regis, 18, 86, 88
  Marshland, 86, 87
  Mildenhall, 5, 20, 22
  Modney, 3, 84
  Mundford, 71
  Narborough, 18
  Oxburgh, 18, 102
  Popham's-ea, 86, 88
  Risby, 22
  Sandwich, 84
  Snorr, 23
  Southerey, 3, 83, 97, 103, 104, 110, 111
  Thetford, 31, 33
  Weeting, 17
  Wereham, 23
  Westley, 16
  West Stow, 71
  Wood Hall (Hilgay), 3
  Ypsilanti, 119
Plantagenet Days, in, Chapter V., 38-57
Play Fields, lack of in country, 99
Political Meetings, 108
Poplot or Powplot, 82, 84, 103

Popular Institutions, Trade Societies, &c., fostered by the Church, 63, 64
Potseye, 12, 15, 22, 82, 115

R.

Rabbits from Muel, 32
Religion—
   Anglican, 79, 80, 81, 93, 97, 98, 103, 104
   British (Christian), 5, 6, 19; (Pagan), 5, 7, 11, 28, 114
   Catholic (Roman), 39, 40, 41, 63, 64
   Nonconformist, 6, 80, 97, 98, 103
   Puritanism, 49, 50-54, 64, 65, 74, 79, 80
   Saxon (Christian), 24-27
Roman terra-cotta ornament, 14
Roman Times, in, Chapter II., 13-20
Roman Villa, disinterred, 5, 14, 18
Roads, 19, 103

S.

Sacred stones, 28
Sam's Cut, the. See Waters
Satirists, Mediæval, 46
Saxons, early ingress of, 21
Schools. See Education
Slusham (Sleves-holm or St. Olaf's-holm), 22, 28, 82, 84, 100
Social conditions compared, 5, 9, 58, 59, 60, 62, 68, 69, 72-74, 76, 80, 108
Social gatherings, 108
Statute-fairs (Statters). See Fairs
Stone, the Settlement, 5
Sunday, the keeping of, 97, 98
Superstitions surviving, 114, 115
Swift, Rev. Thos. See Persons

T.

Technical education. See Education
Tudor Times, in, Chapter VI., 58-78
Turf, use of, as fuel, 122

U.

Unclosed lands, 118

V.

Verse, Dedication; also, 56, 96, 123
Vestry Meetings, 105-107
Village clubs, 105
Vicarage, the Old. See Architecture
Vents (Wents, Wynch, Gwent), 12, 14, 108, 115

W.

Warenne's, the De, residence, 34-36
Waters. Streams, pools, canals, &c., mentioned—
   Buntings streamlet (dry), 2, 3, 4, 8, 9, 20, 32, 36
   Feltwell, 17, 83, 85
   Hoggard's-dyke, 14
   Linnett, 16
   Nar, 17
   Ouse, Little, 17, 82, 84-88
   Ouse, Great, 82-85, 88
   Pottisford, 12, 13, 22, 82
   Popham's-ea, 86, 88
   Sam's Cut, 17, 84, 85
   Wissey, 17, 82, 84, 87
   Wilton stream, 17

Words explained, &c.—
 Acre, 8
 Bon or Bone, 7, 11
 Brent, 7
 Burgh, 13, 18, 30
 Bunting, 26
 By, 22
 Dag, 10
 Dock, 3
 Eldern, 4, 24
 Eye, 12, 16
 Felt, 5, 82
 Folgate, 117
 Gedge, 102
 Grew, 7, 8, 26
 Gwent, 12
 Harde, 87
 Harst, 82 (map)
 Holme, 12-15, 22-27
 Humble, 14

Words explained, &c.—
 Huns, 15
 Hythe, 82 (map)
 Loke, 13
 Mel, 4, 24, 32
 Ottering, 23, 82, 83
 Ouse, 82
 Pit, 3, 13, 24
 Quant, 13
 Set, 9, 71
 Statters, 118
 String, 13
 Suck, 15
 Tennis, 13, 17
 Vents, 12, 14, 17
 Vic, 17
 Wissey, 82

Y.
Younge or Young.   See Persons

AGAS H. GOOSE, PRINTER, RAMPANT HORSE STREET, NORWICH.

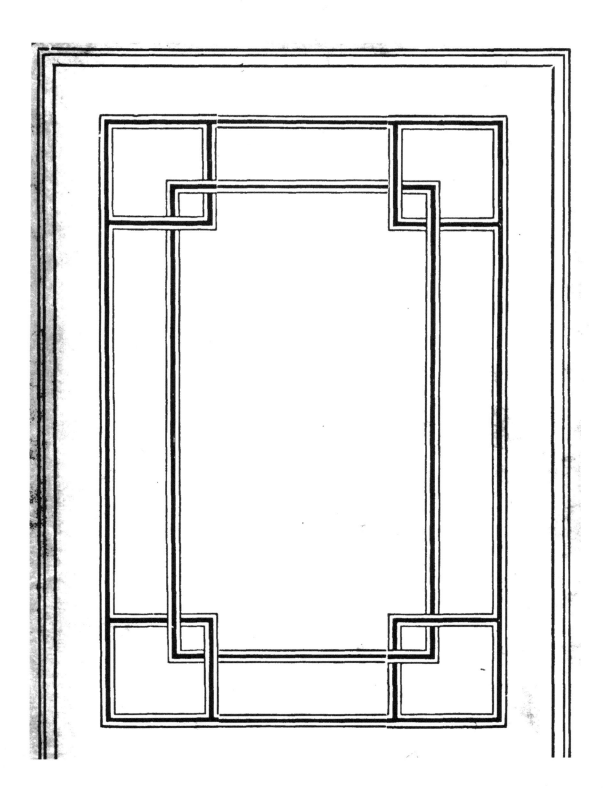

Lightning Source UK Ltd.
Milton Keynes UK
UKHW05f1604180918
329097UK00007B/814/P